To

dr Levy &

with best wishes.

Indrani
Shreekant

To

dr Levy &

with best wishes.

Indrani
Shreekant

INDIAN COOKING

HAMLYN

I   n   d   i   a

A c k n o w l e d g m e n t s

Editor: Penny Summers
Art Editor: Sara Kidd
Designer: Robin Dodd
Production Controllers: Janet Slater, Helen Seccombe

Special Photography: Paul Grater
Food Preparation: Mandy Wagstaff
Styling: Sarah Wiley
Illustrations: Olivia Bown

The publishers wish to thank the following for providing
photographs for this book:
Octopus/Paul Grater page 13, 17, 19, 20, 29, 49, 52, 61, 63;
Octopus/Martin Brigdale page 9, 15, 25, 27, 33, 34, 37, 41, 43, 47, 50, 59;
Octopus/Robert Golden page 23, 31, 38, 45, 55, 57;
Robert Harding Picture Library page 5, 7.

First published 1989 by
The Hamlyn Publishing Group Limited
a division of the Octopus Publishing Group
Michelin House
81 Fulham Road
London SW3 6RB

ISBN 0 600 56542 4

Typeset by J&L Composition Ltd, Filey, North Yorkshire
Produced by Mandarin Offset
Printed and bound in Hong Kong

Contents

INDIAN COOKING

T he chapters in this book are divided according to the types of dishes or the main ingredients rather than the different regional styles. Regional dishes can be identified through the various culinary techniques used. These range from the barbecue-style tandoori food of northern India and Pakistan, where meat is marinated before cooking, to the rich, slow-cooked curries of the Mughal-influenced Delhi school. Central India has created drier vegetable dishes that cook in a matter of minutes, whereas further south the dishes become hotter and coconut is frequently added. At the southern tip of the sub-continent there are the fiery concoctions of Madras, while the coastal and delta regions have developed spicy *masalas* for coating fish prior to baking or charcoal grilling. Hinduism is the predominant religion of India and most Hindus are vegetarians. Sikhs and Muslims, however, enjoy meat as an essential part of their everyday diet. Despite these and other basic differences, such as the fact that Muslims do not eat pork and Hindus do not eat beef, the same basic rules of balanced diet apply all over the Indian sub-continent. From a humble meal of rice, vegetables and pulses, to a magnificent banquet, the emphasis with all Indian food is very much on balance.

Opposite: *the fertile soil of the Kashmir Valley is perfect for growing rice.*

The Traditional Indian Meal

As a general rule, an Indian meal usually consists of several different dishes which are placed on the table together. The diners help themselves to as little or as much as they want, in whatever order they fancy. There is usually a choice of one meat or fish dish or sometimes both, depending on the wealth of the family and the type of occasion, plus several different vegetable dishes, some kind of bread or rice, yogurt, a salad, and a selection of chutneys, relishes and similar accompaniments. In the case of a vegetarian meal, the number of vegetable dishes is increased – lentils and/or another pulse dish are included – and yogurt is always served. Cooking styles, techniques and ingredients obviously vary from one region and religion to another, but it is true to say that Indian meals are always balanced in terms of colour, flavour and, above all, texture. If meat or fish is cooked in a 'wet' sauce, for example, the cook will ensure that there is at least one 'dry' vegetable dish to provide contrast. This is a simple, commonsense rule to apply when you are making up an Indian menu at home.

How Many Courses?

There ar no hard and fast rules when it comes to deciding which dishes to serve. Indian custom is to offer a selection of different dishes from which guests make their choice. Indians do not traditionally eat one course after another, but if you prefer to follow a Western-style pattern of eating with Indian food, then by all means do so – Indian food is extremely adaptable. Foods such as *samosas*, *pakoras* and *dosas*, for example, which are normally eaten throughout the day as snacks in India, make the most appetizing starters for a dinner party, and are now traditionally served as such in Indian restaurants in the West. The 'main course' can then follow with a selection of different curries, tandoori dishes and vegetables, served together with a selection of accompaniments. Due to the scarcity of meat and fish and the large number of vegetarians in India, vegetables are always regarded as dishes in their own right. When planning an Indian meal, they should not be served as accompaniments as they usually are in the West, but should be given equal importance with the meat and fish dishes. Desserts are normally reserved for celebrations and feasts in India, and sweetmeats are eaten throughout the day as snacks rather than to mark the end of a meal, but there is no reason why Indian sweet dishes cannot be offered as Western-style desserts.

Ingredients

The poorer classes of all religions eat mostly vegetarian food, reserving meat for special celebrations and holidays. Even the more humble Indian food is imaginative – over the centuries the poorer people have learnt to make use of the basic foods, such as the numerous varieties of pulse, turning them into tasty dishes simply by the addition of a few spices.

The availability of raw materials is as important as religious beliefs in determining the Indian diet. In the northern regions of Pakistan and Nepal, the Himalayan foothills provide lush grassy slopes for grazing. Here, broad-leaved vegetables, including spinach and cauliflower are grown. Further south on the plains of India, a combination of the baking sun and extensive irrigation encourages the cultivation of peas, beans, lentils and tropical vegetables, such as green peppers, aubergines and bhindi (okra). It is here, too, that the flavouring spices are grown – especially turmeric and chillies. Around the Indian coastline, as yet unspoilt by pollution, seafood, including all manner of shellfish, is abundant. In Bangladesh, the rivers teem with every kind of fish, including the huge *ma sher*, which is large enough to provide a feast for a village.

Rice and Bread

Carbohydrate in the form of rice or bread is a central part of every Indian meal, no matter what the occasion, as it forms the staple diet for the vast majority of Indians. Quite apart from this, however, rice and bread are essential for providing contrast to hot and spicy foods – something that most Westerners will appreciate.

In India, the eating of both rice and bread together is frowned upon, although the choice does not normally arise – bread is eaten more in the north where vast areas of wheat are grown, whereas rice is eaten in the paddy-growing areas of southern India.

When planning an Indian meal at home, rice is certainly the easier choice. Most Indian breads must be freshly cooked to be enjoyed at their best, and this can be tricky if you are entertaining guests and do not want to be confined to the kitchen before the meal. If you are serving rice, observe the Indian rule of spooning only a small amount on to individual plates, then grouping portions of the other dishes around it so that guests can take a little rice with each mouthful of meat, fish or vegetables, etc. Never mound rice up in the centre of the plate and pour curry over it.

How to Serve and Eat Indian Food

It is the Hindu tradition to serve food on a *thali*, a circular metal tray or plate, although in some parts of southern India food is eaten off banana leaves. The *thali* is rather like an artist's palette in that small portions of each dish are arranged around the edge, either in small bowls or directly on the tray, then the diner uses the centre of the tray to eat off, mixing and blending different flavours, colours and textures according to individual choice. Obviously it would be impractical to serve food in this way in a Western home, but, to give an Indian meal a touch of authenticity, encourage your guests to use their plates in the same way as a *thali*, grouping helpings of different dishes around a portion of rice.

Throughout the Indian sub-continent, it is traditional to eat with the right hand. The left hand is never used to touch food because it is considered unclean. Nowadays, however, many Indians use cutlery to eat their food, and when serving Indian food by all means provide dessertspoons and forks, at least for the main course. If you are serving bread, encourage your guests to break it with their fingers and then use it to scoop up their food – they will be surprised how easy it is and how good the food tastes.

Regional Cooking Styles and Techniques

In the north, particularly northern Pakistan, tandoori cooking has dominated for centuries. The *tandoor*, or

A feast of fruit, sweetmeats and vegetables are offered at this sun worship festival.

clay oven, is conically shaped like a beehive. Three hours before cooking, a charcoal fire is lit in the *tandoor* and cooking only begins when searing temperatures are reached inside. Tandoori recipes depend therefore upon quick cooking. Meat is cut into chunks and marinated, then cooked on skewers in a matter of minutes. Poultry is treated in the same way, either whole or cut into serving pieces.

As the *tandoor* is an oven and not merely a charcoal barbecue, it offers one of the few opportunities for making leavened bread. Normally, Indian bread is a simple griddle-cooked dough of flour and water. *Naan*, however, cooked on the inside walls of the *tandoor*, is lighter than most unleavened bread.

Advanced though tandoori cooking is, it is not a complete cuisine. It has developed alongside the Mughal style of cooking, after the fashion of the Mughal emperors who laid great emphasis on presentation. It is within this style, which extends down towards central India, that food appears to be at its most appetizing. From Mughal cooking a new and different style developed around Delhi. This Delhi style is today much revered and many of the best recipes can be found throughout the sub-continent. Bombay, being a major port, developed a more cosmopolitan style, with such delicacies as cutlets and sweet and sour dishes – learnt from the Chinese. Also on the west coast, Indian Christians developed their own styles, particularly in Goa. Further south on the Keralanese coast, the use of fenugreek has been developed to a fine art, mainly to absorb odour in fish dishes.

It seems to be the rule that the hotter the temperature, the hotter the food. Certainly the Madrasis, who live in constantly high temperatures, prove the point. Vindaloo, cooked with the addition of vinegar, has been treated with reverence by generations of restaurant goers in the West.

Cooking Utensils
No special equipment is really required for Indian cooking – the sub-continent is poor, and food often has to be prepared and cooked in primitive conditions. The average Western kitchen is therefore more than well equipped to cope with the demands of Indian cuisine. For example, grinding spices in a mortar and pestle is a much easier operation than using a stone and slab! Currying is basically a stewing process, so a large, heavy-based saucepan is all that is needed. *Bhoona* is similar to the Chinese stir-frying, performed in a wok. A deep-sided frying pan can normally be used for this or, where larger quantities are called for, a heavy-based saucepan.

Obviously a *tandoor* can present a few problems, but a charcoal barbecue will cook marinated meat on skewers. Chicken is best started in a conventional oven and finished on the barbecue. *Naan* is more difficult, but reasonable results can be obtained in a hot oven. Unleavened breads, such as *chapattis*, are traditionally cooked on a dome-shaped disc known as a *tawa*, which is heated over a fire. This utensil is perhaps worth investing in if you intend to cook such dishes frequently, although good results can be obtained using any flat metal plate. When the recipe requires deep-frying – *pakoras*, *puris*, *hoppers*, for example – you can use a normal deep-fat fryer and do not have to buy any special equipment.

What to Drink with Indian Food
Tea is the universal drink in India, served sweet and milky. Other popular drinks include sweet concoctions based on essences, such as sandalwood and mint, and a yogurt drink called *lassi*. With an Indian meal at home, you will probably find the most suitable drinks are ice-cold water, chilled lager or a light beer; fine wines are not appropriate.

7

Special Ingredients

Ata or chapatti flour: This type of wholemeal flour is used to make Indian unleavened breads. Wholemeal flour can be used as a substitute.

Aniseed: These liquorice-flavoured seeds are widely used in the preparation of confectionary and sweet and hot chutneys.

Besan or chick pea flour: This is a very fine yellow flour made from ground chick peas. It should be sieved before use as it tends to form hard lumps during storage. It is low in gluten and very high in protein.

Cardamom: There are two varieties, large and small. The large variety has a black pod and black seeds inside. The seeds of the small green variety impart a pleasant scented flavour and are mostly used for Indian sweets, pilaos and biryanis. The large variety is seldom used for puddings but both varieties are a main ingredient in the making of garam masala. Unless otherwise specified, the cardamoms are used whole and ground with their pods. The ground form is often available in Indian stores.

Channa dal or chick peas: Channa dal are one of India's most popular and versatile pulses. Channa dal are also ground into the fine flour known as *besan* (q.v.).

Chapatti: This type of unleavened bread is made with *ata* or chapatti flour (q.v.), a coarse-textured wheat flour.

Chillies: These are available both fresh and in powder form and in different coloured varieties which vary in strength. The seeds are particularly hot and may be discarded. Prepare chillies under running cold water, wash your hands immediately afterwards and never allow the volatile oils to touch the face, as they can cause painful stinging.

Coconut: Both the meat and the milk of the coconut are used extensively in Indian cookery. A fresh coconut should feel heavy and sound full of juice when the nut is shaken. The 'eye' should be dry and free from mould. After breaking open the shell, the coconut meat can be prized away. Coconut juice is not coconut milk; it is not used in cooking but does make a refreshing drink. To make 450 ml (¾ pint) coconut milk and cream: empty 225 g (8 oz) unsweetened desiccated coconut into a food processor or blender, pour over 450 ml (¾ pint) boiling water and process for 20 to 30 seconds. Turn into a large bowl and add an extra 150 ml (¼ pint) hot water. Leave to cool, then strain the coconut milk through a fine sieve (lined with muslin if possible), squeezing the coconut to extract the milk. Cover and store in the refrigerator; the coconut cream will quickly rise to the surface and can be skimmed off for separate use if required. For extra convenience, it is now possible to buy coconut milk in cans and cartons or as a powder to be made up with water.

Coriander: This is known as *dhania* in India. The leaves

are the most widely used part of the plant. The seeds and powder are also used extensively. It is available at Continental and Indian specialist stores. Parsley can be

1) Bay leaves; 2) Fresh coriander leaves; 3) Bitter gourd; 4) Curry leaves; 5) Pilao rice (page 54); 6) Coconut; 7) Tarka Dal (page 23); 8) Palm sugar; 9) Crystallized sugar; 10) A selection of Indian sweets, including Halwa (page 63) and Barfi (page 62); 11) Aubergines; 12) Tamarind pulp; 13) Indian savoury snacks; 14) Almonds; 15) Raeta (page 53); 16) Cinnamon sticks; 17) Bombay duck; 18) Beetle nut; 19) Mace; 20) Nutmeg; 21) Black cardamom; 22) Green cardamom; 23) Cardamom seeds; 24) Pistachio nuts; 25) Cloves; 26) Sesame seeds; 27) Pomegranate seeds; 28) Cinnamon bark; 29) Fenugreek seeds; 30) Saffron; 31) Indian spicy snack with fennel and aniseed; 32) Dried red and fresh green chillies; 33) Curry powder; 34) Ground turmeric; 35) Indian spicy snack with fennel and aniseed; 36) Poppadoms; 37) Saag Roti (page 55); 38) Paprika; 39) Garam masala; 40) Split green lentils; 41) Chick peas; 42) Split black gram; 43) Brown lentils; 44) Red lentils; 45) Black gram; 46) Yellow lentils.

substituted for the chopped fresh leaves, although it will not impart the same flavour.

Cumin: The seeds resemble caraway but are slightly bitter in taste. Cumin is added to curry powders and garam masala. Whole seeds are used for pilao, vegetable curries and chutneys.

Curry leaves: These are the green leaves of a tree found in India, Pakistan and Sri Lanka, which are used for flavouring and then removed before serving. Green and dry forms are available.

Fenugreek: The yellow seeds are used in curry powders and are slightly bitter. The leaves from the plant resemble clover and are eaten as a leafy vegetable in India. Fresh fenugreek can be grown in the garden from seed.

Full-fat milk powder: This is used in many Indian sweet recipes as a substitute for *khoa* (milk condensed by slow boiling). Baby milk formula is suitable, but skimmed milk powder is not.

Garam masala: This blend of ground spices is used in many savoury dishes. It can be bought ready-made but tastes fresher if made at home. To make garam masala, dry-fry the following spices for 5 to 6 minutes: 1 tablespoon coriander seeds, 1 tablespoon cumin seeds, 2 teaspoons cardamom seeds, 2 teaspoons cloves, 2 teaspoons mace, 7.5 cm (3 inch) cinnamon stick, 1 tablespoon black peppercorns and 1 teaspoon grated nutmeg. Grind the spices to a fine powder in a mill or mortar and pestle and store in an airtight jar.

Ghee: Clarified butter can be heated to a higher temperature than butter and most oils without burning and is widely used in Indian cookery. For the best flavour, *ghee* is made from unsalted butter. A vegetable *ghee* substitute is also available.

To make 175 g (6 oz) *ghee*: melt 225 g (8 oz) butter in a saucepan. Slowly simmer the melted butter until it becomes clear and a whitish residue settles at the bottom. Remove from the heat, spoon off any foam, and allow to cool. Drain the clear oil from the top into a container, straining if preferred. Discard or add the residue to curries for flavouring.

Ginger: Fresh root ginger is sometimes referred to as 'green ginger'. It is peeled before using, then sliced, crushed or chopped finely. To keep fresh: peel, then wash and place in a jar; cover with pale dry sherry, seal and store in the refrigerator. Ground ginger is not an acceptable substitute, but dried root ginger may be used, in which case the quantity should be decreased as it is sharper in taste.

Ginger and garlic pastes: Since many meat, fish and poultry preparations need garlic and/or ginger paste it is very useful to prepare large quantities of each and store them. Both pastes can be safely kept with or without refrigeration for 3 to 4 weeks without change in the taste and flavour. Buy 100 to 175 g (4 to 6 oz) ginger root or garlic cloves, and peel them. The process is made easier if the ginger is soaked overnight. Chop the ginger into small pieces. Grind the garlic or ginger with the minimum of water necessary to make a fine paste. Add about 1.25 ml (¼ teaspoon) salt and mix well. Store wrapped in a polythene bag and placed in a sealed container. Avoid storing either of these pastes too close to other foods.

Guava: The skin of the guava fruit varies from yellow to purple and the flesh from pale green to pink. They are available fresh or canned in syrup.

Kalonji or black onion seeds: These small, tear-shaped onion seeds are used to add piquancy to vegetable curries and Indian breads.

Karela or bitter gourd: This is often used in vegetable curries. It has an ugly, knobbly appearance and is available fresh or canned.

Mango powder: Slices of unripe green mango are used in India as a souring agent when lemons, limes and tamarind are not available. Fresh, unripe green mangoes are peeled, stoned, cut into thin slices and dried in the sun, then processed into a powder, which amongst other uses makes a convenient substitute for tamarind pulp.

Pulses: There are about 60 varieties of pulse available in India. They are dried beans, peas and lentils and the most popular varieties used in Indian cooking include chick peas, split black chick peas, black gram, red lentils and yellow lentils. Pulses should be rinsed in several changes of water and pre-soaking usually reduces the cooking time by half. Salt tends to harden pulses and should not be added until the end of the cooking time. The more unusual varieties are sold in health food and Asian food stores.

Rice: Without exception, rice is the staple food of India and the Orient. Basmati is the most expensive Indian rice, prized for its length of grain and aromatic flavour. Patna is another popular variety.

Rice flour: Made from ground rice, this can be prepared at home using an electric blender, coffee mill, food processor or mortar and pestle.

Rose water: Available from chemists, this is used for flavouring many Indian dishes and has a delicate fragrance. The essence is more expensive.

Saffron: Saffron is used for its exquisite flavour and as a colouring agent for pilaos, biryanis, sweets, puddings and cakes. Gathered from the orange stamens of a type of crocus flower, thousands of fronds are needed to produce a very small amount. To make a solution of saffron for colouring: wrap the saffron fronds in a small polythene bag and crush with a rolling pin, or use a pestle and mortar. Transfer the saffron to a cup and pour the specified amount of hot water or milk over it. Leave it for 10 minutes and stir well with a spoon. For a large pinch of saffron fronds use 50 to 85 ml (2 to 3 fl oz) water or milk.

Tamarind: This acidic fruit resembles a bean pod and is usually sold dried or pulped. It must be made into tamarind water before using: soak about 25 g (1 oz) tamarind pods in 300 ml (½ pint) warm water for at least 5 to 10 minutes (the longer the tamarind is left to soak, the stronger the flavour). The pulp should be squeezed and the liquid strained before use.

Turmeric: The saffron-yellow ground form of turmeric is most commonly used. It is sometimes used to colour a dish but because of its distinctive flavour should only be used when it is specified in the ingredients for a particular recipe.

Urhad dal: The seeds of this Indian pulse are usually sold as lentils. Ground *urhad dal* are used to make poppadoms.

Varak or silver leaf: A popular decoration for both sweet and savoury dishes, this thin silver leaf is safe to eat. Aluminium foil should never be used as a substitute.

10

Menus

Tandoori Lunch

Chick Pea Flour Fritters
Tandoori Chicken
Aubergine with Tomatoes
Rice with Stock and Spices
Charcoal-grilled Fish
Leavened Bread with Poppy Seeds
Mint-flavoured Sauce
Indian Ice Cream with Pistachios

Vegetarian Lunch

Spiced Chick Peas
Rice with Vegetables
Curried Okra
Lentil Sauce with Hot Topping
Vermicelli Pudding

Kebab Party

Chick Pea Flour Bread with Spinach
Marinated Cubes of Lamb
Minced Beef on Skewers
Barbecued King Prawns
Mint-flavoured Sauce
Yogurt with Cucumber or Tomato
Rice
Indian Salad

Seafood Celebration Meal

Steamed Lentil Cakes
Fish Ball Curry
Prawn Curry with Coconut
Spinach with Tomatoes
Potato and Cauliflower Curry
Fried Unleavened Bread
Cream Cheese in a Sweet Cream Sauce

Vegetarian Feast

For 8 to 10 people
Chick Pea Flour Fritters
Rice with Vegetables
Green Lentils
Banana Curry
Stuffed Aubergines
Aubergine with Tomatoes
Dry-fried Spinach
Mint-flavoured Sauce
Yogurt with Cucumber or Tomato
Mango Ice Cream
Honey Squares

Curry Supper

Ground Meat Patties
Lamb with Yogurt and Tomatoes
Curried Okra
Rice
Deep-fried Milk Pastry in Thick Syrup

11

NOTE: Adjust quantities of individual dishes according to the number of people being served.

Ṣnacks

Throughout the Indian sub-continent it has always been the custom to offer snacks and sweetmeats to guests as a sign of welcome. The snacks can range from deep-fried morsels made from semolina or chick pea flour to delicious envelopes of crisp pastry with dry curry fillings and quite substantial spiced meat kebabs. These sweet and savoury titbits are tremendously popular and are sold throughout India by street vendors in the bustling bazaars.

On the whole, Indian snacks are quite easy to make. To be served at their best, many should be eaten freshly cooked, although some may be prepared in batches and stored in airtight containers.

Indian-style Scrambled Eggs

Ekoori

6 eggs
50 g (2 oz) ghee
1 medium onion, peeled and thinly sliced
1 clove garlic, peeled and thinly sliced
10 cm (4 inch) piece fresh root ginger, peeled and cut into thin strips
1 teaspoon turmeric
1 teaspoon garam masala
½ teaspoon chilli powder
1 teaspoon salt
4 fresh green chillies, cored, seeded and chopped into 5 mm (¼ inch) pieces
hot toast, to serve
chopped fresh coriander leaves, to garnish

Whisk the eggs in a bowl and set aside. Melt the ghee in a heavy-based saucepan, add the onion and garlic and fry gently for 4 to 5 minutes until soft. Add the strips of fresh ginger and fry gently for a further 2 minutes until softened, stirring constantly.

Add the turmeric, garam masala, chilli powder and salt to the mixture and cook gently for a further 1 minute, stirring constantly.

Whisk the eggs once again and add to the saucepan. Cook over a gentle heat as for scrambled eggs, scraping the egg from the side of the pan until the mixture is soft and creamy. Remove from the heat immediately, as the eggs will continue cooking in the heat of the pan and it is important not to overcook them.

Sprinkle the chopped chillies into the egg, then fold gently to mix. Pile the scrambled egg on to slices of hot toast and sprinkle with chopped coriander leaves. Serve immediately. *Serves 4*

Note: This is a breakfast-time favourite, although it is equally good served in the afternoon. The technique is very similar to scrambling eggs Western style, and, no doubt, the traditional way of serving it on toast is very much a Western import.

Variations: As an alternative, try serving Ekoori on freshly made Thin Spiced Pancakes/Dosas (page 14). Or make it a more substantial dish by adding 225 g (8 oz) peeled prawns with the onion and garlic. Cooked mussels or clams could also be used; so too could flaked crab meat.

Indian Curd Cheese; Indian-style Scrambled Eggs; Prawn and Egg Sambal

Indian Curd Cheese

Panir

1.2 litres (2 pints) creamy milk
juice of 1 lemon or 4 tablespoons natural yogurt

Put the milk in a large, heavy-based saucepan and bring to the boil. Reduce the heat and add lemon juice or yogurt, which will make the milk curdle.

Stir gently for up to 1 minute, until the curds separate from the whey. As the curd begins to form, stir very gently so that the curds remain in large lumps and do not break up into small pieces. Turn off the heat immediately.

Pour the mixture into a large sieve or colander lined with several thicknesses of muslin. Hold under a gently running cold tap for a few seconds.

Bring up the 4 corners of the muslin and tie together. Twist gently to extract as much moisture as possible, then hang the bag up and leave the cheese to drain for 1½ hours, until crumbly.

To make into Panir, place the cheese, still in the muslin bag, on a work surface and shape into a rectangle. Cover with a board and weight down. Leave for 2 hours, then cut into squares. *Serves 4*
Note: Cheese has never had a following in the Indian sub-continent. However, Panir — a simple curd cheese — is a well-established dish.

Prawn and Egg Sambal

Jhinga Sambal

500 g (1 lb) peeled prawns
4 hard-boiled eggs, shelled and quartered
300 ml (½ pint) coconut milk
1 small onion, peeled and minced
1 clove garlic, peeled and crushed
1 fresh green chilli, cored, seeded and chopped
juice of ½ lemon
pinch of chilli powder
½ teaspoon salt

To garnish:
50 g (2 oz) cooked green peas
chopped fresh coriander leaves

Arrange the prawns and eggs in a shallow serving dish, then chill in the refrigerator.

Place the coconut milk, onion, garlic, chilli, lemon juice, chilli powder and salt in a blender and purée until smooth and evenly mixed. Pour over the prawn and egg mixture. Garnish with the peas and chopped coriander. Serve well chilled, with Poppadoms (page 50), if liked. *Serves 4*
Note: This dish is good for a light buffet or cocktail party. It is simple to make, but full of flavour.

Spiced Chick Peas

Channa Dal

500 g (1 lb) chick peas (channa dal)
1 teaspoon salt
2 teaspoons bicarbonate of soda
2 litres (3½ pints) cold water
vegetable oil for deep-frying
1 tablespoon garam masala
2 teaspoons chilli powder
1 teaspoon freshly ground black pepper
2 teaspoons salt
2 teaspoons raw cane or soft brown sugar

Wash the chick peas thoroughly. Put the salt and bicarbonate of soda in a large bowl, pour in the cold water and stir until dissolved. Add the chick peas and leave to soak for 48 hours.

Drain the chick peas and wash thoroughly in fresh cold water. Drain once more, then spread out on a baking tray and allow to dry in a preheated cool oven (150°C/300°F, Gas Mark 2) for about 30 minutes.

Heat the oil in a deep-fat fryer until one of the chick peas immediately starts to sizzle and float to the surface when dropped into the pan. Deep-fry the chick peas a few at a time until they start to change colour, then remove with a perforated spoon and drain on paper towels while frying the remainder.

Put the warm chick peas in a large jar with the spices, salt and sugar. Shake until all the chick peas are evenly coated. *Makes about 500 g (1 lb)*
Note: These are particularly popular amongst cinema-goers in India. Whereas in the West popcorn is the great cinema snack, in India it is Channa Dal. As the process of making Channa Dal involves quite a lot of time by way of soaking the chick peas, it is worth cooking a reasonable amount at one time. Although best eaten within 1 day of making, they will keep for up to 2 weeks in an airtight container.

Thin Spiced Pancakes

Dosas

175 g (6 oz) Basmati rice
100 g (4 oz) lentils
2 litres (3½ pints) cold water
2 teaspoons salt
½ teaspoon turmeric
300 ml (½ pint) milk
about 100 g (4 oz) ghee for shallow-frying

Mix the rice and lentils together and wash thoroughly. Drain, place in a large bowl and add the water. Leave to soak for 24 hours.

Drain off the water and grind the rice and lentils finely in a blender or food processor. Sprinkle in the salt and turmeric, then pour in the milk to make a batter, whisking well.

Melt a little of the ghee in a shallow, heavy-based frying pan, then pour in enough batter to cover the bottom of the pan, allowing it to spread to the edges. Cook on one side only until the centre becomes solid, then slide out of the pan on to a warmed serving plate. Repeat with the remaining batter, adding more ghee as necessary.

Serve hot, with a selection of chutneys. Alternatively, eat Dosas with Ground Meat Patties/Shami Kebab (page 15) or Indian-style Scrambled Eggs/Ekoori (page 12). *Makes 10 to 15*
Note: These pancakes are usually eaten freshly cooked at breakfast. They make use of the two most freely available ingredients in India: rice and lentils. Traditionally, Dosas are cooked on a heated flat stone, but an ordinary shallow frying pan will serve the same purpose. If liked, 50 to 100 g (2 to 4 oz) chopped coriander or spinach leaves, or 1 teaspoon caraway seeds or aniseed, may be whisked into the batter before cooking.

Chick Pea Flour Fritters

Pakoras

175 g (6 oz) natural yogurt
75 g (3 oz) chick pea flour (besan)
2 teaspoons salt
1 teaspoon chilli powder
1 teaspoon garam masala
½ teaspoon turmeric
½ teaspoon freshly ground black pepper
1 long aubergine, weighing about 500 g (1 lb), or
about 12 large spinach leaves
600 ml (1 pint) vegetable oil for deep-frying

Put the yogurt in a medium bowl and sift in the chick pea flour, whisking it in well. (The flour tends to form quite hard lumps; these need to be pressed through a sieve with the back of a spoon.) Add the salt, chilli powder, garam masala, turmeric and black pepper and mix in well. Place the bowl in a cool place for at least 1 hour (during this time the flour will absorb the moisture from the yogurt and the mixture will become quite stiff).

Trim the aubergine, but do not peel. Cut the aubergine into 2.5 cm (1 inch) cubes. Heat the oil in a deep, heavy-based frying pan until a small drop of the batter immediately starts to sizzle and float to the surface when dropped into the pan. Coat the pieces of aubergine with the batter; it does not matter if the aubergine is not totally coated. Deep-fry the fritters in batches in the hot oil until they are golden brown, about 3 minutes. Remove with a perforated spoon and drain on paper towels.

If you are using spinach leaves, remove the hard central rib from any of the larger leaves, then cut the leaves into 5 cm (2 inch) squares. Coat with the batter and fry in the same way as the aubergine slices. Serve hot, as soon as possible after cooking. *Makes about 12*
Note: Chick pea flour is far more absorbent than ordinary wheat flour, which means that very small amounts can be mixed with quite a considerable amount of liquid to form a very thick batter. Both savoury and sweet fillings can be used — try mushrooms, or apples and bananas. Pakoras will keep for up to 1 hour in a warm oven.

14

Spiced Chick Peas; Chick Pea Flour Fritters; Ground Meat Patties; Thin Spiced Pancakes;
Chick Pea Flour Bread with Spinach (page 55)

Ground Meat Patties

Shami Kebab

50 g (2 oz) ghee
2 medium onions, peeled and thinly sliced
2 cloves garlic, peeled and thinly sliced
4 fresh green chillies, cored, seeded and chopped
2 teaspoons freshly ground black pepper
2 teaspoons chilli powder
2 teaspoons garam masala
1 teaspoon ground cumin
½ teaspoon ground cinnamon
2 teaspoons salt
100 g (4 oz) chick peas (channa dal), soaked in 1 litre
(1¾ pints) cold water overnight
750 g (1½ lb) minced lamb or beef
2 tablespoons chopped fresh coriander leaves
1 egg, beaten
vegetable oil for shallow-frying

To garnish:
1 large onion, peeled and sliced into thin rings
fresh coriander leaves
2 tomatoes, cut into wedges
1 lemon, cut into wedges

Melt the ghee in a large, heavy-based saucepan, add the onions, garlic, chillies, spices and salt and fry gently for about 4 to 5 minutes. Drain the chick peas, add to the pan and cover with fresh cold water. Bring to the boil, then cover the pan and simmer for 1 hour or until tender. Increase the heat and add the minced meat, stirring constantly until the meat is thoroughly cooked and all the liquid has been absorbed. Allow to cool.

Grind the mixture to a fine paste with a hand grinder or in a food processor. Mix in the chopped coriander, then chill in the refrigerator for 30 minutes.

Divide and form into about 10 patties and coat in the beaten egg. Heat the oil in a deep, heavy-based frying pan until hot, add the patties and shallow-fry, in batches, until golden brown, turning once. Garnish with onion rings, coriander leaves, tomato and lemon wedges before serving. *Makes about 10*
Note: Shami Kebabs can form quite a substantial snack – often a meal in themselves. They are a little time-consuming to prepare, but worth the effort.

'Pepper Water' Curry Soup

Mulligatawny

50 g (2 oz) dried tamarind
1.2 litres (2 pints) beef stock
50 g (2 oz) ghee
1 large onion, peeled and sliced
2 cloves garlic, peeled and sliced
1 teaspoon ground ginger
2 teaspoons freshly ground black pepper
2 teaspoons ground coriander
½ teaspoon ground fenugreek
½ teaspoon chilli powder
½ teaspoon turmeric
½ teaspoon salt

Put the dried tamarind in a pan, add just enough of the beef stock to cover, then bring to the boil. Remove the pan from the heat, cover and leave the tamarind to soak for 4 hours.

Melt the ghee in a large, heavy-based pan, add the onion and garlic and fry gently until soft, about 4 to 5 minutes. Add the spices and salt and fry for 3 minutes, stirring constantly. Stir in the remaining beef stock. Strain the liquid from the tamarind through a wire sieve into a clean bowl, rubbing the pulp and seed against the mesh, then discarding the seeds. Add the tamarind juice to the pan and simmer for 15 minutes. Taste and adjust the seasoning before serving. Serve hot. *Serves 4*

Note: Mulligatawny soup has no history in India before the British Raj – it was simply an invention to satisfy the needs of British army officers who demanded a soup course at dinner.

Steamed Lentil Cakes

Bhalli

350 g (12 oz) red lentils
1.75 litres (3 pints) cold water
1 teaspoon ground cumin
1 teaspoon chilli powder
1 teaspoon salt
½ teaspoon freshly ground black pepper
25 g (1 oz) fresh coriander leaves, chopped
juice of 1 lemon
225 g (8 oz) natural yogurt

Wash the lentils thoroughly. Drain, place in a large bowl and add the cold water. Leave to soak for 36 hours.

Drain off the water and grind the lentils to a fine paste in a blender or food processor. Using muslin or a strong tea towel, squeeze the excess water from the lentils. Transfer the paste to a bowl and mix in the cumin, chilli powder, salt, pepper and coriander leaves. Shape into 6 to 8 cakes, 5 cm (2 inches) in diameter and 1 cm (½ inch) thick. Pat them dry with kitchen paper towels.

Place the cakes in the top of a steamer, cover and steam for 1 hour. If you do not have a steamer, place the cakes in a shallow dish, stand the dish in a roasting tin filled with enough hot water to come halfway up the sides of the dish. Cover the dish and tin with foil, then place the tin in a preheated moderately hot oven (190°C/375°F, Gas Mark 5) and cook for 1 hour. Remove the lentil cakes when they are cooked and then allow them to cool completely.

Mix the lemon juice into the yogurt. Put the lentil cakes in a shallow dish and cover with the yogurt mixture. Marinate in the refrigerator for at least 2 hours before serving. *Makes 6 to 8*

Note: This is a very popular dish to eat in the heat of the afternoon. Although quite complicated to make, it is well worth the effort.

Fried Semolina Cakes

Suji Karkarias

225 g (8 oz) semolina
750 ml (1¼ pints) milk
175 g (6 oz) soft brown sugar
75 g (3 oz) ghee, melted
20 cardamoms
10 cloves
25 g (1 oz) shelled pistachios, chopped
3 eggs
vegetable oil for deep-frying

Put the semolina in a bowl and slowly add the milk, mixing well with a spoon to avoid lumps forming. Sprinkle in the brown sugar, add the ghee and mix again until evenly incorporated.

Transfer the mixture to a large, heavy-based saucepan and bring slowly to the boil, stirring constantly. Continue to boil gently until the mixture has the consistency of very thick custard, then remove the pan from the heat and set aside to cool.

Meanwhile, place the cardamoms in a mortar and pestle with the cloves. Grind together until both are reduced to a fairly coarse powder, then mix in the chopped pistachios, but do not grind any further.

Break the eggs one by one into the cold semolina and whisk them into the mixture. Sprinkle in the cardamoms, cloves and pistachios.

Heat the oil in a deep, heavy-based frying pan until a small spoonful of the mixture immediately starts to sizzle and float to the surface when dropped into the pan. Test several times to ensure that the oil is the right temperature. Drop dessertspoonfuls of the mixture into the hot oil and fry in batches until golden brown. Remove with a perforated spoon and place on paper towels to drain while frying the remainder. Serve while slightly warm or leave to cool completely. *Makes 20*

Note: Semolina, made from hard durum wheat, gives these cakes their characteristic crisp texture. The combination of sweetness and crispness makes them a good accompaniment to lemon tea. They will keep fresh for up to 1 week in an airtight container.

Curried Pastries; 'Pepper Water' Curry Soup; Steamed Lentil Cakes

Curried Pastries

Samosas

Pastry:
225 g (8 oz) plain flour
50 g (2 oz) ghee
½ teaspoon salt
150 ml (¼ pint) milk (approximately),
soured with a little lemon juice
vegetable oil for deep-frying

Filling:
Spiced Minced Beef/Keema (page 29)

To make the pastry, sift the flour into a bowl, rub in the ghee, then add the salt. Gradually add the soured milk and mix to make a firm dough which is velvety to the touch. Chill in the refrigerator until required.

Divide the dough into about 12 pieces, each about 2.5 cm (1 inch) in diameter. Roll each out into a very thin circle, then cut each circle in half. Spoon a little of the spiced minced beef mixture in the centre of each semi-circle, then fold in three to make a triangular cone shape, enclosing the filling. Moisten the edges of the dough with a little of any remaining or extra soured milk, then press together to seal.

Heat the oil in a deep, heavy-based frying pan until a samosa immediately starts to sizzle and float to the surface when dropped into the pan. Fry in batches for about 1 minute until the pastry is cooked and golden brown. Remove with a perforated spoon and place on paper towels to drain while frying the remainder. Serve warm. *Makes about 24*

Note: Samosas keep quite well in an airtight container; reheat under a preheated grill until hot before serving.

Crisp Rice Pancakes

Hoppers

2 tablespoons desiccated coconut
200 ml (⅓ pint) cold water
225 g (8 oz) Basmati or Patna rice
½ teaspoon bicarbonate of soda
½ teaspoon salt
25 g (1 oz) butter

Soak the coconut in the water for 4 hours. Meanwhile, grind the rice using a mortar and pestle, blender or food processor.

Strain the coconut water into the ground rice, then add the bicarbonate of soda and salt. Beat well to make a smooth batter, then leave to stand for 12 hours to allow the ground rice to absorb the liquid.

Beat the batter well to incorporate as much air as possible. Lightly grease a hot, deep, frying pan with a little of the butter. Pour in a little of the batter, just enough to cover the bottom of the pan and tilt so that the batter spreads to the edge. Cook on one side only for about 30 seconds or until the centre of the pancake becomes solid, then slide out of the pan on to a warmed serving plate. Repeat this procedure with the remaining batter, greasing with more butter as necessary. Serve hot. *Makes 25 to 30*

Note: Hoppers are fine rice pancakes. Traditionally, they are cooked in round-bottomed earthenware pans called chatties, in the ashes of a charcoal fire. Rice flour batter is poured into a hot chatty and immediately spun so that the batter flies to the curved sides of the vessel and sizzles into a delicate filigree. However, in Western kitchens a deep frying pan with curved sides can be used instead.

17

Vegetable & Pulse Dishes

This chapter includes a pleasing variety of vegetarian dishes and illustrates how important it is to make them lively and interesting by incorporating a good blend of colours, textures and flavours. The Vegetarian menus on page 11 show how the recipes can be served together to make an attractive and appetizing meal.

Braised Okra with Chillies

Bhindi Foogath

50 g (2 oz) ghee
1 large onion, peeled and sliced
3 cloves garlic, peeled and sliced
5 cm (2 inch) piece fresh root ginger,
peeled and finely chopped
2 fresh green chillies, cored, seeded
and finely chopped or minced
½ teaspoon chilli powder
500 g (1 lb) okra, topped and tailed
200 ml (⅓ pint) water
salt
2 teaspoons desiccated coconut

Melt the ghee in a large, heavy-based saucepan, add the onion, garlic, ginger, chillies and chilli powder and fry gently for 4 to 5 minutes until soft, stirring occasionally.

Add the okra, water and salt to taste. Bring to the boil, then lower the heat, cover and simmer for 5 to 10 minutes until the okra are just tender, but still firm to the bite. Stir in the coconut and serve hot. *Serves 4*
Note: Originally from southern India, a Foogath is very similar to a Sambal in that it is a savoury dish made from vegetables. The difference between the two is that the Foogath is cooked and is often made with leftover vegetables. Also, in a Foogath the flavour of ginger is predominant.

Peas with Indian Cheese Curry

Matar Panir

100 g (4 oz) ghee
500 g (1 lb) Indian Curd Cheese/Panir (page 13),
cubed
1 onion, peeled and sliced
1 teaspoon ground ginger
½ teaspoon ground cumin
½ teaspoon chilli powder
½ teaspoon salt
500 g (1 lb) frozen peas
2 tomatoes, chopped

Melt the ghee in a medium frying pan, add the cubed cheese and fry until browned on all sides. Remove with a perforated spoon, drain on paper towels and set aside.

Add the onion to the frying pan and fry gently for 4 to 5 minutes until soft. Add the spices and salt and fry for a further 3 minutes, stirring constantly.

Add the peas and tomatoes and stir gently until the peas are coated with the spice mixture. Stir in the reserved cheese and heat through, taking care not to break up the cubes of cheese. Serve hot. *Serves 4*
Note: This is a basic recipe for an Indian curd cheese curry. The spices used are so light that they will not mask the flavour of the cheese. Other vegetables can be used rather than peas and tomatoes, if liked.

Braised Okra with Chillies; Peas with Indian Cheese Curry

19

Egg and Coconut Curry

Narial Anday

1 fresh coconut
600 ml (1 pint) boiling water
100 g (4 oz) ghee
1 large onion, peeled and thinly sliced
2 cloves garlic, peeled and thinly sliced
2 bay leaves
7.5 cm (3 inch) cinnamon stick
2 teaspoons ground ginger
2 teaspoons chilli powder
1 teaspoon fenugreek seeds
1 teaspoon ground coriander
1 teaspoon ground cumin
1 teaspoon salt
150 g (5 oz) tomato purée
8 hard-boiled eggs, shelled and halved

Make holes in the eyes of the coconut, then drain out the liquid and reserve. Crack open the coconut and separate the meat from the shell. Thinly slice one-third of the meat and set aside.

Put the remaining two-thirds of the meat in a blender or food processor and chop very finely. (Alternatively, finely grate the meat.)

Transfer the chopped or grated coconut to a bowl, pour over the boiling water, stir for 5 minutes, then strain through a sieve lined with a double thickness of muslin held over a bowl. Gather up the muslin and squeeze out as much of the coconut milk as possible. Discard the coconut from inside the cloth. Stir the reserved liquid from the coconut into the coconut milk and set the bowl aside.

Melt the ghee in a large, heavy-based saucepan, add the onion and garlic and fry gently for 4 to 5 minutes until soft. Add the bay leaves, spices and salt; stir well and fry for a further 3 to 4 minutes. Stir in the coconut milk and bring to the boil, adding the tomato purée. Simmer for 5 minutes. Add the sliced coconut and the hard-boiled eggs and heat through gently for a further 2 to 3 minutes. Remove the eggs carefully from the sauce with a perforated spoon and arrange in a warmed serving dish. Pour over the sauce and serve hot. *Serves 4 to 6*

Spinach with Tomatoes; Savoury Rice with Lentils

Potato and Cauliflower Curry

Gobi Mussalum

500 g (1 lb) potatoes
500 g (1 lb) cauliflower
salt
75 g (3 oz) ghee
1 medium onion, peeled and finely chopped
2 cloves garlic, peeled and finely chopped
5 cm (2 inch) piece fresh root ginger,
peeled and finely chopped
2 teaspoons coriander seeds
1 teaspoon black onion seeds (kalonji)
1 teaspoon turmeric
1 teaspoon chilli powder
1 teaspoon freshly ground black pepper
50 g (2 oz) tomato purée
2 teaspoons garam masala

Peel the potatoes and cut into 2.5 cm (1 inch) pieces.

Cut the cauliflower into small florets, discarding any thick stalks. Cook the potato and cauliflower in separate pans of boiling salted water until they just begin to soften, about 5 to 10 minutes.

Meanwhile, melt the ghee in a large, heavy-based saucepan, add the onion, garlic and ginger and fry gently for 4 to 5 minutes until soft. Add the coriander and black onion seeds and fry for a further 30 seconds. Add the turmeric, chilli powder, black pepper and 1 teaspoon salt, stir well and fry for a further 2 minutes. Stir the tomato purée into the mixture.

Drain the potato and cauliflower, reserving a little of the cauliflower water. Add the potato and cauliflower to the saucepan and toss gently in the spice mixture. If the curry is a little too dry, add some of the reserved cauliflower water. Cook for 5 to 6 minutes or until the vegetables are tender, then sprinkle in the garam masala and cook for 1 minute. *Serves 6 to 8*
Variation: For a moist curry, fry the potatoes in the ghee for 1 minute, then remove and set aside. Fry the spices and return the potatoes to the pan with 1 pint water. Simmer for 10 minutes, then add the cauliflower. Simmer until the vegetables are tender and the sauce is thick. Stir in the garam masala and serve hot.

Savoury Rice with Lentils

Kitcheri

350 g (12 oz) Basmati rice
175 g (6 oz) lentils
100 g (4 oz) ghee
1 large onion, peeled and sliced
2 cloves garlic, peeled and sliced
1½ teaspoons turmeric
10 cloves
6 cardamoms
7.5 cm (3 inch) cinnamon stick
salt
1 teaspoon freshly ground black pepper
900 ml (1½ pints) boiling water

Wash the rice and lentils thoroughly, then put in a bowl and cover with cold water. Leave to soak for 2 hours.

Melt the ghee in a large, heavy-based saucepan, add the onion and garlic and fry gently for 4 to 5 minutes until soft. Add the spices, salt to taste and black pepper and fry for a further 3 minutes, stirring constantly.

Drain the rice and lentils, add to the pan and toss for 5 minutes until every grain is coated with the spice mixture. Add the water, bring to the boil, lower the heat, cover with a tight-fitting lid and simmer for 20 to 30 minutes, until the rice and lentils are cooked.

Remove the lid from the pan and boil off any excess liquid before serving, turning constantly to prevent sticking. Serve immediately. *Serves 4*
Note: This is an Indian dish which has become truly international, and today it is hard to think of Kitcheri or Kedgeree as anything other than a means of using up leftovers – usually fish. However, it is a highly-regarded dish in India, particularly on the Keralonese coasts where the seafood Kitcheris are famous. The recipe given is a basic Kitcheri with lentils.

Banana Curry

Kela Kari

50 g (2 oz) ghee
7.5 cm (3 inch) piece fresh root ginger, peeled and thinly sliced
1 tablespoon garam masala
2 teaspoons cumin seeds
1 teaspoon chilli powder
1 teaspoon turmeric
1 teaspoon salt
1 teaspoon freshly ground black pepper
750 g (1½ lb) under-ripe bananas
500 g (1 lb) natural yogurt
juice of 1 lemon
fresh coriander leaves or parsley, to garnish

Melt the ghee in a large, heavy-based saucepan, add the ginger and fry gently for 4 to 5 minutes until soft. Add the garam masala, cumin seeds, chilli powder, turmeric, salt and black pepper. Stir well to mix with the ginger and fry for a further 2 minutes.

Peel the bananas and cut them into 2.5 cm (1 inch) pieces. Add to the pan and turn gently so that they become coated with the spice mixture.

Mix the yogurt and lemon juice together in a bowl, then pour slowly into the pan and mix with the pieces of banana. Bring to just below boiling point, stirring constantly. Reduce the heat and simmer gently for 10 minutes, until the bananas are softened but not broken up. Transfer carefully to a warmed serving dish and serve hot, garnished with fresh coriander leaves or parsley. *Serves 8 to 10*
Note: Bananas are plentiful in India, and often form a substantial part of a vegetarian diet. Be sure to use under-ripe bananas for this curry or they will disintegrate during cooking.

Spinach with Tomatoes

Saag Tamatar

1 kg (2–2¼ lb) fresh spinach
175 g (6 oz) ghee
2 large onions, peeled and thinly sliced
2 cloves garlic, peeled and thinly sliced
150 g (5 oz) fresh root ginger
2 teaspoons chilli powder
2 teaspoons turmeric
2 teaspoons garam masala
2 teaspoons coriander seeds
1 teaspoon ground coriander
1 teaspoon cumin seeds
1½ teaspoons salt
2 teaspoons freshly ground black pepper
1 × 400 g (14 oz) can tomatoes

Wash the spinach and shake it dry. Cut it into strips about 2.5 cm (1 inch) wide, removing any of the thicker stalks. Melt the ghee in a large, heavy-based saucepan, add the onions and garlic and fry gently for 4 to 5 minutes until soft.

Meanwhile, peel the ginger and cut into strips about 3 mm (⅛ inch) thick. Add the ginger to the pan and continue cooking gently for a further 5 to 6 minutes. Add the chilli powder, turmeric, garam masala, coriander seeds, ground coriander, cumin, salt and black pepper, stir well and cook for 1 minute.

Add the spinach and toss to coat in the spice mixture. Add the tomatoes with their juice and bring to the boil, stirring. Add enough boiling water to prevent the spinach sticking to the bottom of the pan. Stir well and simmer for 5 to 10 minutes, until both the spinach and tomatoes are cooked through. Serve hot. *Serves 4 to 6*
Note: Spinach is a very popular vegetable throughout the Indian sub-continent where it has always been noted for its nutritional qualities, as in the West. The type of spinach grown in India tends to be much stronger than that grown in the West; some of it can taste quite bitter, and in order to counteract this, sweet canned tomatoes are added to the dish.

If fresh spinach is not available, frozen spinach can be used, in which case use only half the weight specified for fresh.

21

Dry-fried Spinach

Tali Saag

50 g (2 oz) ghee
1 small onion, peeled and thinly sliced
1 teaspoon garam masala
1 teaspoon salt
500 g (1 lb) fresh spinach,
washed and stalks removed

Melt the ghee in a large, heavy-based saucepan, add the onion and fry gently for 4 to 5 minutes until soft. Add the garam masala and salt and fry, stirring constantly, for 2 to 3 minutes.

Add the spinach and cook for about 5 minutes, stirring constantly. Transfer to a warmed serving dish and serve immediately. *Serves 4 to 6*
Note: Fresh spinach is used in this recipe; if you are using frozen spinach, you will need to halve the quantity specified for fresh.

Curried Okra

Bhindi Bhajji

500 g (1 lb) okra
75 g (3 oz) ghee
1 large onion, peeled and thinly sliced
2 cloves garlic, peeled and thinly sliced
7.5 cm (3 inch) piece fresh root ginger,
peeled and thinly sliced
1½ teaspoons ground cumin
1½ teaspoons turmeric
1 teaspoon ground coriander
1 teaspoon freshly ground black pepper
1 teaspoon salt
100 g (4 oz) canned tomatoes
150 ml (¼ pint) boiling water
1 tablespoon garam masala

Pick over the okra and discard any that are blemished. Wash in cold water, top and tail and cut into 1 cm (½ inch) pieces. Melt the ghee in a large, heavy-based saucepan, add the onion, garlic and ginger and fry gently for 4 to 5 minutes until soft. Add the spices and salt, stir well and fry for a further 3 minutes. Add the okra and turn carefully with a wooden spoon so that they become evenly coated with the spice mixture.

Add the tomatoes with their juice, increase the heat and add the boiling water. Bring to the boil, lower the heat and simmer for about 10 minutes, until the okra are cooked but still crunchy — test by biting into a piece. Sprinkle in the garam masala and stir for a further 1 minute. Serve hot. *Serves 4 to 6*
Note: This vegetable is well known throughout the tropical world, and is found in recipes from the Caribbean right across through India to China. As with most green vegetables okra are best cooked fresh. It is possible to buy them in cans, but both the flavour and texture are sadly lacking. Fresh okra can be recognized by their bright green appearance, the absence of too many black patches on the outside of the vegetable, and the fact that they break cleanly when snapped, with an audible 'pop'. One warning when handling fresh okra: the outer surface is covered with tiny, almost invisible, needle-like spines, which soften on cooking, but can be very painful if they get in your eyes.

Aubergine with Tomatoes

Baigan Tamatar

750 g (1½ lb) aubergines
juice of 1 lemon
175 g (6 oz) ghee
2 medium onions, peeled and thinly sliced
4 cloves garlic, peeled and thinly sliced
7.5 cm (3 inch) piece fresh root ginger,
peeled and thinly sliced
2 teaspoons black onion seeds (kalonji)
7.5 cm (3 inch) cinnamon stick
2 teaspoons coriander seeds
2 teaspoons cumin seeds
2 teaspoons freshly ground black pepper
2 teaspoons salt
2 teaspoons garam masala
1½ teaspoons turmeric
1 teaspoon chilli powder
1 × 400 g (14 oz) can tomatoes
100 g (4 oz) tomato purée
600 ml (1 pint) boiling water
dried red chillies, to garnish

Using a sharp knife, cut the aubergines in half lengthways, then cut again lengthways into quarters. Cut the aubergine crossways at 4 cm (1½ inch) intervals to form chunks. Place in a bowl and mix in the lemon juice.

Melt the ghee in a large, heavy-based saucepan, add the onions, garlic and ginger and fry gently for 4 to 5 minutes until soft. Add the black onion seeds, cinnamon, coriander and cumin and stir well. Fry for a further 2 minutes, then stir in the pepper, salt, garam masala, turmeric and chilli powder.

Add the tomatoes with their juice and the tomato purée, stir well and bring to the boil. Add the boiling water, the aubergine pieces and lemon juice. Bring to the boil, lower the heat and simmer gently for 15 to 20 minutes, until soft. Garnish with the dried red chillies and serve hot. *Serves 4 to 6*
Note: If you have never tried an Indian vegetable dish, then this one is a must. The rich combination of whole tomatoes and concentrated tomato purée greatly enhances the flavour of the aubergines.

When choosing aubergines for this dish, try to select only those which are firm, unwrinkled and deep purple in hue.

Aubergine with Tomatoes; Dry-fried Spinach; Potato and Cauliflower Curry (page 20)

Lentil Sauce with Hot Topping

Tarka Dal

Sauce:
500 g (1 lb) red lentils
50 g (2 oz) ghee
1 medium onion, peeled and thinly sliced
1 clove garlic, peeled and thinly sliced
1½ teaspoons turmeric
½ teaspoon salt
1 teaspoon freshly ground black pepper
1 litre (1¾ pints) water
4 fresh green chillies, cored and seeded

Topping:
2 tablespoons sesame seed oil
4 cloves garlic, peeled and thinly sliced
1 small onion, peeled and thinly sliced
1 teaspoon lovage seeds

Wash the lentils well in cold water. Drain and pick out any stones or discoloured lentils. Melt the ghee in a large, heavy-based saucepan, add the onion and garlic and fry gently for 4 to 5 minutes until soft. Sprinkle in the turmeric, salt and pepper, then add the lentils, stirring well so that they become well coated.

Pour in the water, bring to the boil, then add the whole prepared chillies. Boil for about 20 minutes, stirring from time to time, until the lentils have turned into a yellow sauce, the consistency of a thick custard. (It may be necessary to add more water during cooking, depending on the absorbency of the lentils.) Pour the sauce into a warmed serving dish, cover and keep hot in a preheated moderate oven (180°C/350°F, Gas Mark 4).

To make the topping (*tarka*), heat the oil in a frying pan until smoking. Add the garlic and onion, fry quickly until the garlic blackens, then throw in the lovage seeds. Fry for a further 10 seconds, then pour over the lentil sauce. Serve hot. *Serves 4 to 6*

Note: *Dal*, or lentil sauce, is one of the most commonly found staple dishes throughout the whole of the Indian sub-continent, but the secret of this particular recipe is the topping, which is poured over the sauce prior to serving. The combination of garlic and lovage seeds gives a real piquancy to the dish.

Spinach with Prawns

Saag Jhinga

50 g (2 oz) ghee
1 large onion, peeled and sliced
2 cloves garlic, peeled and sliced
1 tablespoon tomato purée
½ teaspoon garam masala
1½ teaspoons ground coriander
½ teaspoon turmeric
½ teaspoon chilli powder
½ teaspoon ground ginger
1 teaspoon salt
500 g (1 lb) frozen whole leaf spinach
500 g (1 lb) peeled prawns

Melt the ghee in a large, heavy-based saucepan, add the onion and garlic and fry gently for 4 to 5 minutes until soft. Stir in the tomato purée and fry, stirring constantly, for 1 minute. Add the spices and salt and fry for a further 5 minutes, stirring constantly.

Add the frozen spinach and break up with a wooden spoon. Cook until the spinach has thoroughly defrosted, about 3 to 4 minutes, stirring frequently. Add the prawns and cook for a further 5 minutes, turning the prawns gently to coat with the spinach. Serve immediately. *Serves 4*
Note: The combination of spinach and prawns is unusual, yet the two flavours complement each other extremely well.

Rice with Vegetables

Subzi Pilao

225 g (8 oz) frozen diced mixed vegetables
100 g (4 oz) frozen diced red and green peppers
100 g (4 oz) courgettes, trimmed and sliced
2 tablespoons ground cumin
2 tablespoons ground coriander
1 tablespoon chilli powder
2 teaspoons turmeric
4 teaspoons black peppercorns, crushed
2 teaspoons salt
100 g (4 oz) ghee
4 large onions, peeled and thinly sliced
5 cloves garlic, peeled and thinly sliced
2 × 7.5 cm (3 inch) pieces fresh root ginger,
peeled and thinly sliced
2 × 7.5 cm (3 inch) cinnamon sticks
20 cardamoms
20 cloves
1 tablespoon lovage seeds
750 g (1½ lb) Basmati rice
2 litres (3½ pints) boiling water
75 g (3 oz) sultanas
50 g (2 oz) flaked almonds

Mix the frozen vegetables with the courgettes and allow to defrost. Mix together the spices and salt.
Melt half of the ghee in a large, heavy-based saucepan. Add half of the spice mixture and fry gently for 1 to 2 minutes, then add the vegetables and stir to coat in the ghee and spice mixture. Remove the vegetables from the pan with a perforated spoon and place in a bowl. Keep hot in a preheated cool oven (150°C/300°F, Gas Mark 2).

Melt the remaining ghee in the saucepan, add the onions, garlic and ginger and fry gently for 4 to 5 minutes until soft. Add the cinnamon sticks, cardamoms, cloves and lovage seeds, stir well and fry for a further 3 to 4 minutes. Add the remaining spice mixture and fry for 2 minutes.

Wash the rice well in cold water. Drain, then pick the rice over to remove any stones or other 'undesirable' objects. Add it to the saucepan and stir well to ensure it is coated with the spice mixture. Pour in the boiling water and boil gently, uncovered, until the rice is cooked but still firm in the centre, stirring from time to time so that it does not stick. If necessary, add a little more boiling water.

When the rice is ready, pour it into a large sieve and allow any liquid to drain away. Mix with the vegetables and arrange on a warmed serving platter. Sprinkle over the sultanas and almonds and serve immediately. *Serves 6 to 8*
Note: At any vegetarian feast, the rice dish usually forms the centrepiece.

Stuffed Aubergines

Baigan

4–6 medium aubergines, halved lengthways
100 ml (3½ fl oz) water
1 bay leaf
100 g (4 oz) ghee
1 large onion, peeled and finely chopped
2 cloves garlic, peeled and finely chopped
2 teaspoons coriander seeds
1 teaspoon chilli powder
1 teaspoon lovage seeds
1 teaspoon salt

To garnish:
fresh coriander leaves
dried red chillies, chopped

Put the aubergines in a roasting tin with their cut sides upwards. Pour in the water, add the bay leaf and cover the tin tightly with foil. Poach the aubergines in a preheated moderate oven (160°C/325°F, Gas Mark 3) for 25 minutes, or until soft.

Melt the ghee in a heavy-based saucepan. Add the onion and garlic and fry gently for 4 to 5 minutes until soft. Crush the coriander seeds slightly and add to the onion mixture with the chilli powder, lovage seeds and salt. Stir well and fry for a further 2 to 3 minutes.

Remove the poached aubergines from the water and pat them dry with paper towels. Using a sharp-edged teaspoon, scrape out the flesh from inside the skins. Reserve the skins. Mash the aubergine flesh well and add to the spice mixture. Fry for 2 to 3 minutes, stirring well.

Rice with Vegetables; Banana Curry (page 21); Stuffed Aubergines; Green Lentils;
Honey Squares (page 62); Mango Ice Cream (page 60)

Grill the aubergine skins for 5 minutes until dried out, then fill with the fried aubergine mixture. Arrange the aubergines on a warmed serving dish, garnish with the chillies and coriander and serve. *Serves 4 to 6*
Note: For this recipe, use the long variety of aubergine rather than the shorter, rounded ones. As with all aubergine dishes, it is important to select firm, ripe aubergines.

Green Lentils

Moongh Dal

225 g (8 oz) green lentils
900 ml (1½ pints) water
1 teaspoon salt
50 g (2 oz) ghee
1 medium onion, peeled and thinly sliced
2 cloves garlic, peeled and thinly sliced
2 teaspoons garam masala
1 teaspoon turmeric
1 teaspoon chilli powder
1 teaspoon cumin seeds
2 tablespoons chopped fresh coriander leaves

Wash the lentils well and soak them in cold water for about 1 hour. Drain, place in a saucepan with the cold water and the salt. Bring to the boil, then reduce the heat to a gentle simmer and cook for about 1 hour until the lentils have softened. Stir from time to time to prevent the lentils sticking to the bottom of the pan and add more water, if necessary. When the lentils are cooked, keep them hot over the lowest possible heat while frying the spices.

Melt the ghee in a heavy-based frying pan, add the onion and garlic and fry gently for 4 to 5 minutes until soft. Sprinkle in the garam masala, turmeric, chilli powder and cumin seeds, stir well and fry for a further 1 minute. Pour this mixture over the lentils and stir in with half of the chopped coriander. Transfer to a warmed serving dish, sprinkle over the remaining chopped coriander and serve immediately. *Serves 4 to 6*
Note: There are scores of different varieties of lentil to be found in India, but not so many are available in the West. Green lentils can be found at Indian stores and health food shops under the name of brown or continental lentils. They have an unusual 'earthy' flavour and hold their shape well, but if they are not available, ordinary red lentils can be used instead.

Meat Dishes

The word curry comes from the Tamil word *kari* which means 'sauce'. For most of the population of India this thick, dark sauce is very important, as it is the only means by which simple ingredients are given flavour and interest. The sauce is not thickened by flour but is given 'body' by the use of ingredients such as onion, ginger and garlic. The rich brown colour comes from the careful frying of all these ingredients together with the special blend of spices.

Indian 'Scotch Egg' Curry

Nargisi Kofta

7 eggs
500 g (1 lb) minced beef
1½ teaspoons freshly ground black pepper
1 teaspoon salt
2 cloves garlic, peeled and roughly chopped
1 teaspoon ground cumin
1 bunch fresh coriander
vegetable oil for shallow-frying

Sauce:
150 g (5 oz) ghee
4 large onions, peeled and thinly sliced
3 cloves garlic, peeled and thinly sliced
15 cm (6 inch) piece fresh root ginger,
peeled and thinly sliced
1 teaspoon salt
2 teaspoons freshly ground black pepper
1½ teaspoons chilli powder
1½ teaspoons turmeric
150 g (5 oz) tomato purée
600 ml (1 pint) rich beef stock
2 teaspoons garam masala

Hard-boil 6 of the eggs and allow to cool. Mix the minced beef with the black pepper, salt, garlic, cumin and most of the leaves from the bunch of coriander (reserving a few for the garnish). Put through the finest blade of a mincer or chop in a food processor, then bind with the remaining beaten egg. Knead well and divide into 6 portions.

Shell the hard-boiled eggs and shape each portion of minced meat around each one to form a ball. Pour about 1 cm (½ inch) oil into a heavy-based frying pan. Heat the oil until hot, then add the beef-covered eggs and fry gently until golden brown on all sides, about 8 to 10 minutes. Remove from the pan with a perforated spoon and drain on paper towels; keep hot in a warm oven.

To make the sauce, melt the ghee in a large, heavy-based saucepan, add the onions, garlic and ginger and fry gently for 4 to 5 minutes until soft. Add the salt, pepper, chilli and turmeric, stir well and cook for 2 minutes. Stir in the tomato purée and stock and bring to the boil. Boil vigorously for 5 minutes, or until the sauce is reduced to three-quarters of its original volume.

Add the cooked eggs to the sauce and cook very gently for a further 15 minutes. Sprinkle in the garam masala, then stir it evenly into the sauce. Transfer to a warmed serving dish, garnish with the reserved fresh coriander leaves and serve hot. *Serves 6*

Note: The use of eggs in India is, to a certain extent, still regarded as a sign of affluence. This dish, combining minced beef and hard-boiled eggs in a rich tomato sauce, makes an excellent centrepiece for any curry-based meal.

Calcutta Beef Curry

Calcutta Gosht

1 kg (2–2¼ lb) braising steak
1 teaspoon salt
1 tablespoon chilli powder
2 teaspoons ground coriander
1 teaspoon freshly ground black pepper
1½ teaspoons turmeric
1 teaspoon ground cumin
1 litre (1¾ pints) milk
100 g (4 oz) ghee
2 large onions, peeled and thinly sliced
5 cloves garlic, peeled and thinly sliced
7.5 cm (3 inch) piece fresh root ginger,
peeled and thinly sliced
2 teaspoons garam masala

Cut the beef into 4 cm (1½ inch) cubes, being careful to trim away excess fat and gristle. Put the salt and ground spices, except the garam masala, in a large bowl. Mix in a little of the milk to make a paste, then gradually add the remaining milk. Add the cubes of beef to the bowl and turn in the milk and spice mixture until they are evenly coated.

Melt the ghee in a large, heavy-based saucepan, add the onions, garlic and ginger and fry gently for 4 to 5 minutes until soft. Remove the beef from the milk and spice mixture with a perforated spoon, add to the pan and fry over a moderate heat, turning the cubes constantly until they are sealed on all sides.

Increase the heat, add the milk and spice mixture and bring to the boil. Cover the pan, reduce the heat and cook gently for 1½ to 2 hours, or until the beef is tender and the sauce reduced.

Just before serving, sprinkle in the garam masala. Increase the heat and boil off any excess liquid so that you are left with a thick sauce coating the cubes of beef. Transfer the hot curry to a warmed serving dish and serve immediately. *Serves 4 to 6*

Note: This recipe really comes into its own when you have the good-quality meat that is available in the West. In Calcutta, where the recipe originated, it is most frequently made with lamb or goat meat. Using beef brings out the richness of the sauce.

Calcutta Beef Curry; Lamb with Extra Onions (page 31)

27

Madras Beef Curry

Madrasi Kari

500 g (1 lb) braising or stewing beef
100 g (4 oz) ghee
1 large onion, peeled and sliced
3 cloves garlic, peeled and sliced
1½ teaspoons ground coriander
2 teaspoons turmeric
1 teaspoon ground ginger
1 teaspoon ground cumin
2½ teaspoons chilli powder
2 teaspoons garam masala
1 teaspoon salt
1½ teaspoons freshly ground black pepper
200 ml (⅓ pint) water

Cut the beef into 2.5 cm (1 inch) cubes, trimming away all fat. Melt the ghee in a large, heavy-based saucepan, add the beef and fry briskly until browned on all sides. Remove from the pan with a perforated spoon and set aside. Add the onion and garlic to the saucepan and fry gently for 4 to 5 minutes until soft. Add the spices, salt and pepper and fry for a further 3 minutes, stirring constantly.

Return the beef to the pan and fry for a further 3 minutes, stirring the beef to coat with the spices. Stir in the water, bring to the boil, lower the heat, cover and simmer gently for 1½ hours, or until the meat is tender. Serve hot. *Serves 4*
Note: This is one of the hottest beef curries!

Minced Beef with Bitter Gourd

Keema Karela

500 g (1 lb) bitter gourd (karela),
or 1 × 225 g (8 oz) can karela
juice of 1 lemon
100 g (4 oz) ghee
2 medium onions, peeled and thinly sliced
2 cloves garlic, peeled and thinly sliced
7.5 cm (3 inch) piece fresh root ginger,
peeled and sliced
1 teaspoon salt
1½ teaspoons freshly ground black pepper
1 teaspoon chilli powder
1 teaspoon ground cumin
750 g (1½ lb) minced beef
2 teaspoons garam masala

Wash the fresh karela, top and tail, then cut into 1 cm (½ inch) slices. Place the slices in a bowl and sprinkle with the lemon juice. (If using canned karela, drain the brine from the can, then wash the karela once with clean cold water and drain again, making sure not to lose any of the seeds. Place in a bowl and sprinkle with the lemon juice.)

Melt the ghee in a large, heavy-based saucepan. Add the onions, garlic and ginger and fry gently for 2 to 3 minutes, making sure that they do not brown. Add the salt, pepper, chilli powder and cumin. Stir well, then add the minced beef. At this stage it may be necessary to add a little water to prevent the mixture sticking to the bottom of the pan – the quantity of water depends on the water content of the onions and the fat content of the beef. Turn the minced beef continuously until it starts to change colour.

Add the slices of karela together with the lemon juice in which they have been soaking. Reduce the heat and continue to cook gently for about 5 to 7 minutes until the karela is soft. Sprinkle in the garam masala, stir the mixture well to ensure it is well distributed, then cook for a further 2 minutes. Serve hot. *Serves 4 to 6*
Note: Karela is a curious-looking vegetable, long and rather gnarled and bright green in colour. It is easy to obtain from Asian and Caribbean greengrocers in large cities, but if you cannot find it, fresh courgettes may be substituted. Canned karela can also be used.

Meatball Curry

Kofta Kari

500 g (1 lb) minced beef
2 large onions, peeled and chopped
4 cloves garlic, peeled and chopped
2 teaspoons turmeric
2 teaspoons chilli powder
2 teaspoons ground coriander
1½ teaspoons ground cumin
1 teaspoon ground ginger
2 teaspoons salt
1 egg, beaten
vegetable oil for deep-frying
100 g (4 oz) ghee
200 ml (⅓ pint) water
fresh mint or coriander leaves, to garnish

Put the beef in a bowl and add half of the onions, garlic, spices and salt. Stir well to mix, then bind the mixture together with the beaten egg.

Divide and shape the mixture into 12 small balls. Heat the oil in a deep, heavy-based frying pan until very hot, add the meatballs in batches and deep-fry for 5 minutes. Remove with a perforated spoon and place on paper towels to drain while frying the remainder, then set aside.

Melt the ghee in a large, heavy-based saucepan, add the remaining onions and garlic and fry gently for 4 to 5 minutes until soft. Add the remaining spices and salt and fry for a further 3 minutes, stirring constantly. Add the meatballs and turn gently to coat with the spices. Add the water, bring to the boil, lower the heat and simmer gently for 30 minutes. Serve hot, garnished with fresh mint or coriander leaves. *Serves 4*
Note: Minced beef is often used in Indian cooking, and Kofta is a classic method. In this recipe the meatballs are sealed by deep-frying; although this takes a little extra time, it reduces the risk of the meatballs falling apart during cooking.

Meatball Curry; Spiced Beef in Yogurt

Spiced Beef in Yogurt

Pasanda

500 g (1 lb) braising or stewing beef, thinly sliced
1 teaspoon salt
300 ml (½ pint) natural yogurt
175 g (6 oz) ghee
1 large onion, peeled and sliced
3 cloves garlic, peeled and sliced
1½ teaspoons ground ginger
2 teaspoons ground coriander
2 teaspoons chilli powder
½ teaspoon ground cumin
1½ teaspoons turmeric
1 teaspoon garam masala

Put the beef between 2 sheets of greaseproof paper
and beat until thin with a mallet or rolling pin. Rub the
beef with the salt, cut into serving-sized pieces, then
put in a bowl and cover with the yogurt. Cover and leave
to marinate overnight in the refrigerator.

Melt the ghee in a large, heavy-based saucepan, add
the onion and garlic and fry gently for 4 to 5 minutes
until soft. Add the spices and fry for a further 3 minutes,
stirring constantly.

Add the beef and yogurt marinade to the saucepan,
stir well, cover with a tight-fitting lid and simmer for 1½
hours or until the meat is tender. Serve hot. *Serves 4*
Note: This is a fine northern dish. Usually beef is used,
although lamb may be substituted.

Spiced Minced Beef

Keema

50 g (2 oz) ghee
2 large onions, peeled and sliced
2 cloves garlic, peeled and sliced
1 teaspoon turmeric
2 teaspoons chilli powder
½ teaspoon ground coriander
½ teaspoon cumin seeds
1 teaspoon salt
1 teaspoon freshly ground black pepper
500 g (1 lb) minced beef

Melt the ghee in a large, heavy-based saucepan, add
the onions and garlic and fry gently for 4 to 5 minutes
until soft. Add the spices, salt and pepper and fry for a
further 3 minutes, stirring constantly.

Add the beef and fry, stirring frequently, until
browned. Continue frying until the meat is cooked and
the curry is dry, about 10 minutes. Serve hot. *Serves 4*
Note: This is a simple and easy dish to prepare, and is
often used for banquets and other functions. Use the
very best quality minced beef available. If liked, peas or
diced boiled potatoes can be added.

Minced Beef on Skewers

Seekh Kebab

750 g (1½ lb) minced beef
2 large onions, peeled and roughly chopped
4 cloves garlic, peeled and roughly chopped
75 g (3 oz) fresh breadcrumbs
3 tablespoons chopped fresh coriander leaves
2 teaspoons garam masala
2 teaspoons freshly ground black pepper
1½ teaspoons poppy seeds
1½ teaspoons sesame seeds
½ teaspoon chilli powder
1½ teaspoons salt
2 eggs, beaten

To garnish:
lettuce leaves
lime slices
chopped raw onion

Pass the beef, onions and garlic through the finest blade of a mincer, or chop in a food processor. Transfer to a bowl, knead well, then mix in the remaining ingredients. Knead again for 1 minute, then chill in the refrigerator for 30 minutes.

Mould the mixture into sausage shapes about 10 cm (4 inches) long and press on to 6 skewers. (There should be enough mixture to make 12 shapes, 2 on each skewer.) Barbecue or grill gently until cooked (about 10 minutes), turning frequently. Serve hot, garnished with lettuce leaves, lime slices and chopped onion. *Serves 4 to 6*
Note: These kebabs are best cooked on thick metal skewers, to enable the meat to be cooked from the inside as well as the outside.

Dry Beef Curry

Bhuna Gosht

50 g (2 oz) ghee
500 g (1 lb) beef steak, sliced into strips
1 small onion, peeled and sliced
2 cloves garlic, peeled and sliced
1 teaspoon chilli powder
1 teaspoon ground cumin
1 teaspoon garam masala
½ teaspoon freshly ground black pepper
1 fresh red chilli, cored, seeded and sliced
½ teaspoon salt

Melt the ghee in a large, heavy-based frying pan until smoking hot, add the beef and stir briskly for 30 seconds, turning the meat constantly to prevent sticking and burning. Remove the meat from the pan with a perforated spoon and set aside.

Add the onion and garlic to the pan and fry gently for 4 to 5 minutes until soft. Stir in the spices and black pepper and fry for 3 minutes, stirring constantly. Return the meat to the pan, stir in the sliced red chilli and salt

and fry for a further 5 minutes or until the meat is tender. Serve hot, with boiled rice and Yogurt with Cucumber or Tomato/Raeta (page 53). *Serves 4*
Note: Bhuna is a way of cooking by frying. It can be used with meat and vegetables, although it is usual to pre-cook meat unless it is cut into small thin pieces. Usually Bhuna dishes are dry with a little sauce, and the skill in cooking them lies in not using water. However, if this proves too difficult and the meat shows signs of sticking, then you may cheat just a little and add water – providing it is boiled away before serving.

Savoury Rice with Meat

Biryani

350 g (12 oz) Basmati rice
750 ml (1¼ pints) water
2 teaspoons salt
450 ml (¾ pint) Curry Sauce (page 53)
350 g (12 oz) cooked meat (beef, chicken or lamb, for example), cut into 2.5 cm (1 inch) cubes
1½ teaspoons turmeric
½ teaspoon ground coriander

To garnish:
1 green or red pepper, cored, seeded and cut into rings
2 hard-boiled eggs, shelled and sliced
2–3 firm tomatoes, sliced
fresh coriander leaves (optional)
silver leaf (varak), finely beaten (optional)

Wash the rice thoroughly. Bring the water to the boil in a large, heavy-based saucepan; add the rice and salt and bring back to the boil. Simmer for exactly 10 minutes, then drain off the excess water and set the rice aside.

Put the curry sauce in a pan with the cooked meat and heat until hot and bubbling. Add the turmeric and coriander and cook over a high heat for 2 minutes, stirring constantly. Add the rice and stir thoroughly but gently until the rice has absorbed the colour of the turmeric evenly. Cover the pan with a tight-fitting lid, lower the heat and cook gently until the rice is completely cooked, about 15 to 20 minutes.

Transfer the mixture to a warmed serving platter. Garnish with pepper rings, egg and tomato slices. Top with fresh coriander leaves and sprinkle with silver leaf, if liked. Serve immediately. *Serves 4*
Note: The Mughal emperors demanded very high standards in all aspects of their cuisine, and such lowly dishes as rice were not exempt. Biryani was perfected as an attempt to raise the humble rice grain to higher culinary status – and make a rice dish fit for kings!

In India Biryanis often steam for hours over the embers of a charcoal fire, although this is usually more for convenience than necessity, and the intrinsic flavour of the dish is the same when cooked by the above method.

Any type of rice can be used but Basmati is best. A simple Raeta (page 53), salad or chutney is often enough accompaniment and in restaurants a curry sauce is often served as a side dish.

Savoury Rice with Meat

31

Lamb with Extra Onions

Gosht Dopiaza

750 g (1½ lb) boneless shoulder of lamb
5 large onions, peeled
100 g (4 oz) ghee
6 cloves garlic, peeled and thinly sliced
7.5 cm (3 inch) piece fresh root ginger, peeled and thinly sliced
1 tablespoon chilli powder
2 teaspoons ground coriander
2 teaspoons ground cumin
2 teaspoons freshly ground black pepper
1½ teaspoons turmeric
2 teaspoons salt
350 g (12 oz) natural yogurt
300 ml (½ pint) beef stock
6 fresh green chillies, cored, seeded and cut into 5 mm (¼ inch) pieces
1 tablespoon fenugreek seeds
2 tablespoons chopped fresh mint leaves

Cut the lamb into 4 cm (1½ inch) cubes, being careful to trim away excess fat and gristle. Purée 1 onion to a paste in a blender or food processor, then transfer to a bowl. Add the cubes of lamb and mix well together.

Melt the ghee in a large, heavy-based saucepan, add the cubes of lamb and fry until sealed on all sides. Meanwhile, thinly slice the remaining onions. Remove the cubes of lamb from the pan with a perforated spoon and set aside.

Add the onions, garlic and ginger to the pan and fry gently for 4 to 5 minutes until soft. Meanwhile, mix the ground spices and salt with the yogurt. Add the yogurt and spice mixture to the pan, increase the heat and add the lamb, stirring constantly. Add the stock, stir well, and bring to the boil. Cover, reduce the heat and cook gently for 40 minutes. Add the fresh chillies with the fenugreek seeds and mint, then simmer for a further 5 to 10 minutes, or until the meat is cooked through. Serve hot. *Serves 4 to 6*

Note: The Hindu word for onion is *piaz* and the word for two is *do* (pronounced as dough) – therefore Gosht Dopiaza means 'meat with double onions'. Onions form a crucial part of virtually all Indian curry dishes and, in fact, many Indians regard onions as vegetables in themselves.

Lamb Curry

Mhaans Kari

500 g (1 lb) boneless shoulder or leg of lamb
100 g (4 oz) ghee
1 large onion, peeled and sliced
2 cloves garlic, peeled and sliced
2 teaspoons ground coriander
1 teaspoon turmeric
1 teaspoon ground cumin
½ teaspoon freshly ground black pepper
1 fresh green chilli, cored, seeded and chopped
½ teaspoon chilli powder
300 ml (½ pint) water
1 teaspoon salt

Cut the lamb into 2.5 cm (1 inch) cubes, being careful to trim away excess fat and gristle. Melt the ghee in a large, heavy-based saucepan, add the lamb and fry briskly until browned on all sides. Remove from the pan with a perforated spoon and set aside.

Add the onion and garlic to the pan and fry gently for 4 to 5 minutes until soft. Stir in the spices, pepper, chilli and chilli powder and fry for a further 3 minutes, stirring constantly. Return the lamb to the pan, add the water and salt, then simmer for 45 to 60 minutes or until the meat is tender. Cover the pan if a curry with plenty of sauce is preferred; cook uncovered for a dry curry. Serve hot. *Serves 4*

Lamb with Yogurt and Tomatoes

Roghan Gosht

1 kg (2–2¼ lb) boneless shoulder of lamb
juice of 2 lemons
500 g (1 lb) natural yogurt
½–1 teaspoon salt
75 g (3 oz) ghee
2 medium onions, peeled and sliced
4 cloves garlic, peeled and sliced
5–7.5 cm (2–3 inch) piece fresh root ginger, peeled and sliced
2 teaspoons chilli powder
2 teaspoons ground coriander
2 teaspoons ground cumin
1 teaspoon freshly ground black pepper
10 cardamoms
225 g (8 oz) tomato purée
300 ml (½ pint) boiling water

Cut the lamb into 2.5 cm (1 inch) cubes, being careful to trim away all fat and gristle. Put the cubes in a large bowl and sprinkle in the lemon juice. Add the yogurt and salt and stir well to mix. Cover and leave to marinate in a cool place for at least 24 hours, or in the bottom of the refrigerator for up to 3 days. Turn the cubes from time to time to ensure that they are all coated in the marinade.

Melt the ghee in a large, heavy-based saucepan, add the onions, garlic and ginger and fry gently for 4 to 5 minutes until soft. Add the ground spices and pepper, stir well and cook for a further 2 minutes. Add the cardamoms, tomato purée, meat and marinade and bring to the boil, stirring constantly. Add the boiling water, cover and cook for 1 to 1½ hours, until the meat is tender. Serve hot. *Serves 4 to 6*
Note: Roghan Gosht is typical of the lamb cookery in northern India and Pakistan, and this dish has become very well known in the West, thanks mainly to the advent of Tandoori restaurants. This particular recipe contains a substantial quantity of tomato purée, which gives the dish a very deep red sauce.

Marinated Cubes of Lamb

Husseini Kebab

1 kg (2–2¼ lb) shoulder of lamb
juice of 1 lemon
2 teaspoons salt
1½ teaspoons freshly ground black pepper
1 medium onion, peeled
2 cloves garlic, peeled
7.5 cm (3 inch) piece fresh root ginger, peeled
1½ teaspoons chilli powder
225 g (8 oz) natural yogurt
2 teaspoons coriander seeds
2 teaspoons cumin seeds
1 teaspoon aniseed

Bone the meat and trim off all excess fat. Cut the meat into 2.5 cm (1 inch) cubes, place in a bowl and sprinkle with the lemon juice, salt and freshly ground black pepper. Rub this mixture well into the cubes of meat, then set aside.

Place the onion, garlic and ginger in a blender or food processor with the chilli powder and mince finely. Add the yogurt and strain in the juice from the lamb. Blend well, then pour over the lamb.

Cover and leave the lamb to marinate in a cool place for at least 24 hours, turning the cubes over from time to time to ensure that they are all evenly coated in the yogurt marinade.

Meanwhile, spread out the coriander seeds, cumin seeds and aniseed on a baking tray and roast in a preheated moderately hot oven (200°C/400°F, Gas Mark 6) for 10 to 15 minutes. Remove the spices from the oven and leave until cold, then transfer to a mortar and pestle and grind to a fine powder.

Thread the cubes of lamb on to oiled metal kebab skewers and sprinkle over the ground roasted spices. Place the skewers on the preheated grid of the barbecue and cook gently over charcoal until the lamb is tender, turning the skewers frequently so that the meat browns on all sides. Alternatively, cook under a moderate grill. Serve hot. *Serves 4 to 6*
Note: The key ingredients to this dish are the aromatic spices: roasted coriander, cumin and aniseed. It is best to bone the lamb yourself, as most butchers do not remove sufficient fat when boning meat.

Rice with Stock and Spices (page 54); Indian Salad (page 49); Potato and Cauliflower Curry (page 20); Spiced Leg of Lamb

Spiced Leg of Lamb

Raan

3 kg (7 lb) leg of lamb, trimmed of fat
3 lemons
2 teaspoons salt
10 cloves garlic, peeled
2 × 7.5 cm (3 inch) pieces fresh root ginger, peeled
1 teaspoon freshly ground black pepper
1 tablespoon boiling water
5 cm (2 inch) cinnamon stick
10 cloves
seeds of 20 cardamoms
2 tablespoons clear honey
500 g (1 lb) natural yogurt
50 g (2 oz) shelled pistachios
100 g (4 oz) blanched almonds
2 teaspoons chilli powder
1 teaspoon turmeric

Make deep slashes in the lamb with a sharp knife. Place in an ovenproof dish or casserole with a tight-fitting lid.

Cut two of the lemons in half, then rub the cut surfaces over the lamb, squeezing the juice into the slashes in the meat. Sprinkle with the salt and set aside.

Purée the garlic and ginger to a paste in a blender or food processor. Add the pepper, then rub the mixture into the meat. Cover and marinate for 8 hours.

Meanwhile, crush the cinnamon, cloves and cardamom seeds in a mortar and pestle.

Put the honey in a blender or food processor with the yogurt, pistachios, almonds, chilli powder and turmeric. Blend or process until well mixed together, then sprinkle in the crushed cinnamon, cloves and cardamoms. Pour this mixture over the lamb, cover and marinate for a further 8 hours.

Place the covered lamb dish in a preheated hot oven (230°C/450°F, Gas Mark 8) and cook for 10 minutes. Reduce the temperature to moderate (180°C/350°F, Gas Mark 4) and cook for a further 2 hours, basting the meat every 15 minutes or so. Remove the lid of the dish, increase the oven temperature to hot (220°C/425°F, Gas Mark 7) and cook for a further 10 minutes.

This dish can be served hot, straight from the oven, but it is more traditional to serve it after it has cooled for an hour or so. *Serves 8*

m e a t d i s h e s

Royal Lamb Curry

Shahi Korma

1 kg (2–2¼ lb) lean boneless lamb (leg or shoulder)
juice of 1 lemon
225 g (8 oz) natural yogurt
75 g (3 oz) ghee
2 medium onions, peeled and thinly sliced
4 cloves garlic, peeled and thinly sliced
7.5 cm (3 inch) piece fresh root ginger, peeled
and thinly sliced
7.5 cm (3 inch) cinnamon stick
10 cloves
10 cardamoms
2 teaspoons ground coriander
2 teaspoons ground cumin
2 teaspoons chilli powder
1 teaspoon turmeric
1 teaspoon freshly ground black pepper
1½ teaspoons salt
300 ml (½ pint) boiling water
100 g (4 oz) whole blanched almonds
50 g (2 oz) shelled pistachios
150 ml (¼ pint) single cream
silver leaf (varak), to garnish (optional)

Cut the lamb into 4 cm (1½ inch) cubes, being careful to trim away excess fat and gristle. Put the cubes in a bowl, pour in the lemon juice and mix well. Mix in the yogurt, cover and leave the lamb to marinate in a cold place or the refrigerator for at least 2 hours.

Melt the ghee in a large, heavy-based saucepan, add the onions, garlic and ginger and fry gently for 4 to 5 minutes until soft. Add the cinnamon, cloves and cardamoms, stir well and fry for a further 1 minute.

Mix together the ground coriander, cumin, chilli powder, turmeric, pepper and salt. Add to the pan, stir well, and cook for a further 2 minutes.

Add the lamb together with the marinade, stir well to ensure the cubes of meat are well coated in the spice mixture, then stir in the boiling water. Chop half of the almonds and stir into the lamb. Cover the pan and simmer gently for about 50 minutes, or until cooked.

Before serving, sprinkle in the remaining whole almonds and the pistachios, lower the heat and pour in the cream, stirring well to mix. Cook gently for a further 5 to 10 minutes, without allowing it to boil. Transfer to a warmed serving dish, garnish with silver leaf, if liked, and serve hot. *Serves 4*

Spiced Lamb Kebabs

Tikka Kebab

500 g (1 lb) boneless shoulder or leg of lamb
juice of 1 lemon
150 ml (¼ pint) natural yogurt
4 small onions, peeled and quartered
3 cloves garlic, peeled and chopped
½ teaspoon turmeric
1 tablespoon vinegar
½ teaspoon salt
1 teaspoon freshly ground black pepper
1 green pepper, cored, seeded and cut into squares
1 lemon, quartered, to garnish

34

Fried Bread in Saffron and Pistachio Sauce (page 58); Vermicelli Pudding (page 61);
Indian savoury snacks; Royal Lamb Curry

Cut the lamb into 2.5 cm (1 inch) cubes, being careful to trim away excess fat and gristle. Put the lamb in a bowl and sprinkle with the lemon juice. Put the yogurt, half the onion, the garlic, turmeric, vinegar, salt and pepper in a blender or food processor and purée until the mixture is evenly blended. Pour over the lamb and stir well. Cover and leave to marinate in the refrigerator overnight.

To cook, thread the cubes of marinated meat on to kebab skewers, alternating with the green pepper and remaining onion quarters. Barbecue or grill the kebabs, over or under a medium heat, turning frequently, until tender, about 10 minutes.

Serve hot, garnished with lemon quarters, and accompanied by Leavened Bread with Poppy Seeds/ Naan (page 51) and salad. *Serves 4*

Note: A fine northern Indian delicacy, Tikka Kebab can be found over charcoal barbecues at virtually every street corner. Ideally they should be cooked over a charcoal griddle, but satisfactory results can be obtained by grilling.

Hot Pork Curry with Vinegar

Shikar ka Vindaloo

750 g (1½ lb) boneless shoulder of pork
200 ml (7 fl oz) malt vinegar
2 teaspoons salt
4 teaspoons coriander seeds
4 teaspoons cumin seeds
seeds of 20 cardamoms
2 teaspoons black peppercorns
10 cloves
2 teaspoons turmeric
75 g (3 oz) ghee
2 large onions, peeled and thinly sliced
6 cloves garlic, peeled and thinly sliced
7.5 cm (3 inch) piece fresh root ginger, peeled and thinly sliced
5 bay leaves
2 teaspoons chilli powder
2 teaspoons garam masala

Cut the pork into 4 cm (1½ inch) cubes, being careful to trim away excess fat and gristle. Put the cubes in a bowl, pour in the vinegar and sprinkle in the salt. Mix well together, then cover and leave to marinate in a cool place for 2 hours.

Meanwhile, put the coriander, cumin and cardamom seeds in a mortar and pestle with the peppercorns, cloves and turmeric. Grind to a powder, then spoon a little of the vinegar from the pork into the mixture to make a thick paste. Remove the pork from the marinade with a perforated spoon and place in a clean bowl. Reserve the vinegar marinade. Stir the spiced paste into the pork, cover and leave to marinate in a cool place overnight.

Melt the ghee in a large, heavy-based saucepan, add the onions, garlic and ginger and fry gently for 4 to 5 minutes until soft. Add the bay leaves and chilli powder

and stir well to mix. Add the pork cubes, turning continuously to seal them. Increase the heat and add the reserved vinegar marinade. Cover, reduce the heat and cook gently for 1¼ hours, or until the pork is thoroughly cooked and tender. Sprinkle in the garam masala just before serving. Serve hot or chilled. *Serves 4 to 6*

Note: Pork is not very widely eaten in India, for reasons of religion and hygiene. The word *shikar* can mean any animal which has been hunted, but in general it is taken to mean the wild boar traditionally hunted by men on horseback armed with lances. Wild boar is not essential for this recipe — ordinary pork from the butcher will do.

Pork Curry

Shikar Kari

100 g (4 oz) dried tamarind
200 ml (⅓ pint) boiling water
500 g (1 lb) boneless pork
50 g (2 oz) ghee
1 large onion, peeled and sliced
3 cloves garlic, peeled and chopped
2 green chillies, cored, seeded and chopped
1 teaspoon ground ginger
3 cloves
5 cm (2 inch) cinnamon stick
1 tablespoon ground coriander
1 teaspoon turmeric
½ teaspoon chilli powder
½ teaspoon cumin seeds

Soak the tamarind in the water for 2 hours.

Cut the pork into 2.5 cm (1 inch) cubes, being careful to trim away excess fat and gristle.

Melt the ghee in a large, heavy-based saucepan, add the onion and garlic and fry gently for 4 to 5 minutes until soft. Add the chillies and spices and fry for a further 3 minutes, stirring constantly. Add the pork and fry for a further 5 minutes, stirring until each piece of meat is coated with the spice mixture.

Strain the tamarind, discarding the seeds, and stir the water into the pan. Bring to the boil, lower the heat, cover and simmer for about 1 hour or until the meat is tender. Serve hot. *Serves 4*

Note: The tamarind water in this recipe counteracts the fattiness of the pork.

Ç h i c k e n Ḍ i s h e s

Chicken is very popular all over the Indian sub-continent. It is usually skinned and cut up before cooking as this allows the flavour of the spices to penetrate the chicken and the dish is less fatty.

To prepare pieces of poultry for a tandoori dish, deep gashes are made in the flesh which is then coated in the marinade of yogurt and seasonings. The yogurt tenderizes the meat while the gashes allow the flavour to reach deep inside the flesh.

The tandoori method of baking chicken is probably the best known, but there is a wide variety of cooking methods to choose from as you will discover when you try some of the delicious recipes in this chapter.

Rice Cooked with Chicken

Murgh Biryani

4 small onions, peeled and halved
2 bay leaves
1 litre (1¾ pints) water
1.5–1.75 kg (3–4 lb) boiling chicken
½ teaspoon saffron threads
750 g (1½ lb) Basmati rice
100 g (4 oz) ghee
5 cloves garlic, peeled and thinly sliced
10 cloves
10 cardamoms
2 × 7.5 cm (3 inch) cinnamon sticks
50 g (2 oz) blanched almonds
100 g (4 oz) sultanas

To garnish:
4 hard-boiled eggs, shelled and sliced
1 large onion, peeled, thinly sliced and fried
until crisp

Put the onion halves and bay leaves into a large saucepan, pour in the water and bring to the boil. Add the chicken to the pan, cover and simmer gently for 1½ to 2 hours, until the bird is tender.

Remove the chicken from the pan and reserve the cooking liquid and onions. Pull the flesh away from the carcass and discard the skin and bones. Place the flesh in a bowl, cover with foil and keep warm in the bottom of a preheated cool oven (150°C/300°F, Gas Mark 2). Bring 120 ml (4 fl oz) of the reserved cooking liquid to the boil in a saucepan. Put the saffron threads in a cup and pour over the boiling liquid. Leave to soak for 10 minutes.

Meanwhile, wash the rice well; drain, then pick it over to remove any stones or other 'undesirable' foreign bodies.

Melt the ghee in a clean, large, heavy-based saucepan. Remove the onions from the reserved cooking liquid with a perforated spoon and drain. Add to the ghee with the garlic, cloves, cardamoms and cinnamon and fry gently for 5 minutes.

Add the rice and stir well so that each grain is coated in the ghee mixture. Strain in enough of the remaining cooking liquid to cover the rice, then strain in the saffron-coloured liquid and bring to the boil. Cook gently, uncovered, for 10 to 15 minutes until the rice has just softened, adding a little boiling cooking liquid or water if necessary.

When the rice is cooked, drain off any excess liquid, then transfer the rice to a warmed large bowl. Mix in the almonds, sultanas and cooked chicken. Arrange the Biryani on a warmed large platter and garnish with the sliced eggs and fried onion. Serve hot. *Serves 6*
Note: In recent years, Biryani recipes have been adapted as a means of using up leftovers. This classic recipe goes back to first principles.

Barbecued King Prawns (page 46); Minced Beef on Skewers (page 30); Tandoori Chicken

Tandoori Chicken

Murgh Tandoori

8 chicken quarters
juice of 2 lemons
2 teaspoons salt

Marinade:
10 cloves
2 teaspoons coriander seeds
2 teaspoons cumin seeds
seeds of 10 cardamoms
2 medium onions, peeled and chopped
4 cloves garlic, peeled and chopped
7.5 cm (3 inch) piece fresh root ginger,
peeled and chopped
2 teaspoons chilli powder
2 teaspoons freshly ground black pepper
1½ teaspoons turmeric
350 g (12 oz) natural yogurt
orange or red food colouring (optional)

Remove the skin from the chicken pieces and discard. Wash the chicken and pat dry with paper towels. Make deep slashes in each piece with a sharp knife. Put the pieces in a bowl and sprinkle with lemon juice and salt. Rub this mixture in well, then cover the bowl and leave in a cool place for 1 hour.

Meanwhile, prepare the marinade: spread the cloves, coriander, cumin and cardamom seeds out on a baking tray and roast in a preheated moderately hot oven (200°C/400°F, Gas Mark 6) for 10 to 15 minutes.

Remove from the oven and allow to cool, then grind coarsely with a mortar and pestle. Place the onions, garlic and ginger in a blender or food processor and sprinkle with the chilli powder, black pepper and turmeric. Add the yogurt and ground roasted spices, strain in the lemon juice from the chicken and blend well until smooth. Add sufficient food colouring to give a bright colour, if liked.

Arrange the chicken pieces in a single layer in a roasting tin and pour over the marinade. Cover the tin and leave the chicken to marinate in the refrigerator for at least 24 hours, turning the pieces over occasionally.

Transfer the roasting tin to a preheated moderately hot oven (200°C/400°F, Gas Mark 6) and roast for 20 minutes. Transfer the chicken to a barbecue or pre-heated grill and cook until the outside is crisp. Serve hot or cold. *Serves 8*

Note: Tandoori food takes its name from the clay oven or *tandoor* in which the food is cooked. A *tandoor* is not a normal piece of equipment in a Western kitchen, but quite acceptable results can be achieved using a combination of a conventional oven for the main cooking and a charcoal barbecue to finish.

Although whole baby chickens or poussins are traditionally used for Murgh Tandoori, chicken quarters are used here as they lend themselves more readily to barbecue cooking. The beauty of this method is that the chicken can be roasted in the oven several hours in advance, kept in the refrigerator, then finished off on the barbecue.

Double Spiced Chicken

Murgh Masala

4 chicken breasts, skinned and boned
juice of 1 lemon
1½ teaspoons salt
2 teaspoons freshly ground black pepper
1 medium onion, peeled
2 cloves garlic, peeled
5 cm (2 inch) piece fresh root ginger, peeled
350 g (12 oz) natural yogurt

Masala:
75 g (3 oz) ghee
1 medium onion, peeled and thinly sliced
1 clove garlic, peeled and thinly sliced
1½ teaspoons turmeric
1½ teaspoons chilli powder
1 teaspoon ground cinnamon
seeds of 20 cardamoms
2 teaspoons coriander seeds
2 teaspoons aniseed

Cut the chicken meat into strips about 2.5 cm (1 inch) wide, place in a bowl and sprinkle with the lemon juice, salt and freshly ground black pepper. Rub in well, then cover and set aside.

Place the onion, garlic and ginger in a blender or food processor and chop finely. Add the yogurt and strain in the juice from the chicken. Purée until blended, then pour over the chicken. Cover and marinate in the refrigerator for at least 24 hours.

Thread the chicken on to kebab skewers, reserving the marinade. Barbecue or grill as slowly as possible until just cooked through (it is important not to overcook the chicken), about 6 to 8 minutes. Remove the chicken from the skewers.

Meanwhile, make the masala: melt the ghee in a large, heavy-based frying pan, add the onion and garlic and fry gently for 4 to 5 minutes until soft. Sprinkle in the turmeric, chilli and cinnamon, stir well and fry for 1 minute.

Add the cardamom seeds, coriander seeds and aniseed and cook, stirring constantly, for 2 minutes, then add the reserved yogurt marinade. Mix well and bring to the boil. Add the chicken pieces and cook for 2 to 3 minutes. Serve hot. *Serves 4 to 6*

Chicken with Lentils; Hyderabad-style Chicken; Chicken Korma

Hyderabad-style Chicken

Murgh Hyderabad

100 g (4 oz) ghee
1 large onion, peeled and sliced
2 cloves garlic, peeled and sliced
4 cardamoms
4 cloves
2.5 cm (1 inch) cinnamon stick
2 teaspoons garam masala
1 teaspoon turmeric
1 teaspoon chilli powder
1 teaspoon salt
*1.5 kg (3 lb) roasting chicken, skinned, boned and cut
into 8 pieces*
flesh of ½ fresh coconut, thinly sliced
1 tablespoon tomato purée
300 ml (½ pint) water

Melt the ghee in a large, heavy-based saucepan, add the onion and garlic and fry gently for 4 to 5 minutes until soft. Add the spices and salt and fry for a further 3 minutes, stirring constantly.

Add the chicken and fry for 10 minutes until browned on all sides. Add the coconut, tomato purée and water. Stir well to mix and bring to the boil, then lower the heat, cover with a tight-fitting lid and simmer for 45 minutes or until the chicken is cooked and tender. Serve hot. *Serves 4*
Note: This recipe, from Hyderabad, Deccan, uses coconut, and it is well worth buying a fresh one to make it, if at all possible.

Chicken with Lentils

Murgh Dhansak

*500 g (1 lb) dried split beans or lentils
(ideally channa dal and moong dal)*
1.2 litres (2 pints) water
175 g (6 oz) ghee
2 large onions, peeled and sliced
4 cloves garlic, peeled and sliced
6 cloves
6 cardamoms
1½ teaspoons ground ginger
2 teaspoons garam masala
2½ teaspoons salt
*1.5 kg (3 lb) roasting chicken, skinned, boned and cut
into 8 pieces*
500 g (1 lb) frozen whole leaf spinach
4 large tomatoes, chopped

Wash the split beans or lentils, place in a saucepan and add the water. Bring to the boil, cover and simmer for 15 minutes.

Meanwhile, melt the ghee in a large, heavy-based saucepan, add the onions and garlic and fry for 4 to 5 minutes until soft. Add the spices and salt and fry for a further 3 minutes, stirring constantly.

Add the chicken and fry until browned on all sides, then remove from the pan with a perforated spoon and drain on paper towels.

Add the spinach and tomatoes to the pan and fry gently for 10 minutes, stirring occasionally.

Mash the beans in their cooking water, then stir into the spinach mixture. Return the chicken to the pan, cover with a tight-fitting lid and simmer for 45 minutes or until the chicken is cooked and tender. Serve hot.
Serves 4
Note: The Parsees are a people who trace their origins back to antiquity and Murgh Dhansak is a dish which dates almost as far back. Literally translated, it means 'wealthy chicken'.

Strictly speaking, this dish should be made from equal quantities of two types of pulse – channa dal and moong dal (available from specialist shops). If these are not available, use whichever dried split bean or lentil is most readily available.

Chicken Korma

Kookarh Korma

175 ml (6 fl oz) natural yogurt
2 teaspoons turmeric
3 cloves garlic, peeled and sliced
*1.5 kg (3 lb) roasting chicken, skinned and cut
into 8 pieces*
100 g (4 oz) ghee
1 large onion, peeled and sliced
1 teaspoon ground ginger
5 cm (2 inch) cinnamon stick
5 cloves
5 cardamoms
1 tablespoon crushed coriander seeds
1 teaspoon ground cumin
½ teaspoon chilli powder
1 teaspoon salt
1½ tablespoons desiccated coconut
2 teaspoons roasted almonds

Put the yogurt, turmeric and 1 clove garlic in a blender or food processor and purée to mix evenly. Place the chicken pieces in a shallow dish and pour over the yogurt mixture. Cover and place in the refrigerator to chill overnight.

Melt the ghee in a large, heavy-based saucepan, add the onion and remaining garlic and fry gently for 4 to 5 minutes until soft. Add the spices and salt and fry for a further 3 minutes, stirring constantly.

Add the chicken pieces with the yogurt marinade and coconut and mix well. Cover with a tight-fitting lid and simmer for 45 minutes or until the chicken is cooked and tender.

Transfer to a warmed serving dish and scatter over the almonds. Serve hot. *Serves 4*
Note: This is one of the most famous Indian dishes, which makes good use of the marinating process. The Korma method can also be applied to meat; Lamb Korma is particularly popular in northern India.

Variation: Alternatively, the chicken may be cooked whole; allow an extra 20 to 30 minutes' cooking time.

39

Whole Spiced Baked Chicken

Murgh Mussalum

1 tablespoon coriander seeds
1 tablespoon cumin seeds
2 bay leaves
1.5 kg (3 lb) roasting chicken
100 g (4 oz) thick natural yogurt
1 medium onion, peeled and roughly chopped
3 cloves garlic, peeled and roughly chopped
3 fresh green chillies, cored, seeded and
roughly chopped

Roasting mixture:
100 g (4 oz) ghee
1 large onion, peeled and thinly sliced
2 cloves garlic, peeled and thinly sliced
7.5 cm (3 inch) piece fresh root ginger, peeled
and thinly sliced
5 cm (2 inch) cinnamon stick
10 cloves
10 cardamoms
2 teaspoons black peppercorns
2 teaspoons salt
150 ml (¼ pint) chicken stock
2 teaspoons garam masala

To garnish:
fresh coriander leaves
lemon wedges

Spread the coriander seeds, cumin seeds and bay leaves on a baking tray. Roast in a preheated moderately hot oven (200°C/400°F, Gas Mark 6) for 10 to 15 minutes, until the bay leaves are crisp. Meanwhile, skin the chicken and wash well. Pat the chicken dry with paper towels, then make deep slashes in the leg and breast meat with a sharp knife.

Put the yogurt, onion, garlic and fresh chillies in a blender or food processor and purée until smooth. Grind the roasted seeds and bay leaves together with a mortar and pestle and add to the yogurt mixture. Rub this mixture over the chicken, then leave to marinate in a cool place for 24 hours, basting the chicken from time to time with the yogurt mixture.

When ready to cook the chicken, make the roasting mixture: melt the ghee in a flameproof casserole with a close-fitting lid. Add the onion, garlic and ginger and fry gently for 4 to 5 minutes until soft. Gently pound the cinnamon, cloves, cardamoms and peppercorns with a mortar and pestle and add to the casserole. Sprinkle in the salt, then add the chicken stock and bring to the boil. Add the garam masala, stirring well, then add the chicken together with the marinade. Cover tightly, increase the heat and shake the casserole continuously for 2 minutes.

Transfer the casserole to a preheated moderately hot oven (190°C/375°F, Gas Mark 5) and cook for 1 hour. Remove the casserole from the oven and increase the oven temperature to hot (230°C/450°F, Gas Mark 8).

Remove the bird from the casserole and place in a roasting tin. Baste with some of the sauce from the casserole, then roast in the oven for about 30 minutes, or until the outside of the chicken is crisp and the juices run clear when the thickest part of a thigh is pierced with the point of a sharp knife.

When the remaining juices from the casserole have cooled slightly, pour into a blender or food processor and purée until smooth, then reheat. Serve the chicken hot, garnished with coriander and lemon wedges. Serve the juices as a sauce in a separate bowl. *Serves 4*
Note: This is one of the tastiest of hot Indian chicken dishes. As with virtually all chicken recipes from India, it makes use of poultry that has been skinned rather than plucked. It seems the simple reason for this is that Indian butchers have always regarded plucking far too time-consuming, and prefer to remove the skin and feathers together when they draw the bird. Skinning a chicken is fairly straightforward, but if you are not sure how to set about it, your butcher should help you.

Chicken Curry

Kukul Kari

100 g (4 oz) ghee
1 large onion, peeled and sliced
3 cloves garlic, peeled and sliced
4 fresh green chillies, cored, seeded and chopped
2 teaspoons ground coriander
1½ teaspoons turmeric
1.5 kg (3 lb) roasting chicken, skinned and cut
into 8 pieces
600 ml (1 pint) coconut milk
juice of ½ lemon

Melt the ghee in a large, heavy-based saucepan, add the onion and garlic and fry gently for 4 to 5 minutes until soft. Add the chillies and spices and fry for a further 3 minutes, stirring constantly.

Add the chicken pieces to the pan and fry gently for 10 minutes until browned on all sides. Stir in the coconut milk and simmer for 45 minutes or until the chicken is cooked and tender.

Add the lemon juice and simmer for a further 10 minutes, stirring occasionally. Serve hot. *Serves 4*
Note: There is a multitude of recipes for Chicken Curry; this one is from Sri Lanka.

Whole Spiced Baked Chicken

Fish &
Shellfish

The fish cooking of India is often overlooked, yet this vast country, with its extensive coastline, rivers and lakes, boasts an enormous variety of fish and seafood. Many of the coastal regions are noted for their fish dishes and each year a festival is held to give thanks for all the goodness supplied by the sea.

Prawn Curry

Jhinga Kari

50 g (2 oz) ghee
1 small onion, peeled and sliced
2 cloves garlic, peeled and sliced
2 teaspoons ground coriander
½ teaspoon ground ginger
1 teaspoon turmeric
½ teaspoon ground cumin
½ teaspoon chilli powder
2 tablespoons vinegar
500 g (1 lb) peeled prawns
200 ml (⅓ pint) water
chopped fresh coriander leaves, to garnish

Melt the ghee in a large, heavy-based saucepan, add the onion and garlic and fry gently for 4 to 5 minutes until soft.

Mix the coriander, ginger, turmeric, cumin and chilli powder to a paste with the vinegar, then add to the pan and fry for a further 3 minutes, stirring constantly.

Add the prawns and turn gently with a wooden spoon until coated with the spices. Stir in the water, then simmer over a gentle heat for 2 to 3 minutes.

Serve immediately, with plain boiled rice and garnished with coriander leaves. *Serves 4*
Note: Prawns are plentiful in the Indian sub-continent, particularly in coastal areas. Most of the best recipes come from Kerela in the south west, where cooks realize the importance of not masking the delicate flavour of the prawns.

Fish Ball Curry

Muchli Kari

750 g (1½ lb) white fish fillets (haddock or cod)
juice of ½ lemon
1 egg
2½ teaspoons salt
freshly ground black pepper
50 g (2 oz) chick pea flour (besan)
4 fresh green chillies, cored, seeded and finely chopped
1 medium onion, peeled and finely chopped
2 tablespoons breadcrumbs
vegetable oil or ghee for shallow-frying

Sauce:
100 g (4 oz) ghee
1 large onion, peeled and thinly sliced
2 cloves garlic, peeled and thinly sliced
7.5 cm (3 inch) cinnamon stick
2 bay leaves
2 teaspoons ground cumin
2 teaspoons ground coriander
1½ teaspoons turmeric
1 teaspoon chilli powder
150 g (5 oz) tomato purée
600 ml (1 pint) chicken stock
juice of ½ lemon
50 g (2 oz) desiccated coconut
seeds of 10 cardamoms
2 teaspoons fenugreek seeds
fresh coriander leaves, to garnish

Arrange the fish fillets in an ovenproof dish and sprinkle with the lemon juice. Cover the dish with foil and stand in a roasting tin. Pour in enough hot water to come halfway up the sides of the dish, then poach in a preheated moderate oven (160°C/325°F, Gas Mark 3) for 15 minutes, or until the fish is fully cooked. Remove the dish from the roasting tin and allow the fish to cool.

Whisk the egg in a medium bowl with 1½ teaspoons salt and pepper to taste. Sift in the chick pea flour, whisking all the time to make a smooth batter. (The flour tends to form quite hard lumps at this stage; these need to be pressed through the sieve with the back of a spoon.)

Flake the fish into the bowl, discarding the skin and any bones. Add the chillies, onion and breadcrumbs to the batter to form a stiff paste. Break off lumps about the size of an apricot and form into balls – there should be sufficient to make about 20. Heat the oil or ghee in a deep, heavy-based frying pan and shallow-fry the balls in batches until they are uniformly brown. Remove from the frying pan with a perforated spoon, drain on paper towels and keep hot in a warm oven.

To make the sauce, melt the ghee in a large, heavy-based saucepan, add the onion and garlic and fry gently for 4 to 5 minutes until soft. Add the cinnamon, bay leaves, cumin, coriander, turmeric and chilli, stir well and cook for a further 2 minutes. Stir in the tomato purée, increase the heat and bring to the boil, slowly stirring in the chicken stock and lemon juice. Sprinkle in 1 teaspoon salt and the coconut, then boil the sauce gently for 10 minutes.

Grind the cardamom and fenugreek seeds with a mortar and pestle. Sprinkle into the sauce, reduce the heat and add the fish balls. Simmer for 5 minutes. Transfer to a warmed serving dish, garnish with coriander leaves and serve hot. *Serves 4 to 6*

Fish Ball Curry

43

Madras Dry Prawn Curry

Jhinga Kari Madrasi

50 g (2 oz) ghee
1 small onion, peeled and sliced
2 cloves garlic, peeled and sliced
1 teaspoon ground coriander
½ teaspoon turmeric
pinch of ground ginger
½ teaspoon ground cumin
½ teaspoon salt
500 g (1 lb) peeled prawns
1 tablespoon vinegar
pinch of chilli powder, to garnish

Melt the ghee in a large, heavy-based saucepan, add the onion and garlic and fry gently for 4 to 5 minutes until soft. Add the spices and salt and fry for a further 3 minutes, stirring constantly.

Reduce the heat to very low, then add the prawns and toss lightly for 1 minute until coated with the spices. Stir in the vinegar, then increase the heat and cook for 30 seconds.

Sprinkle with the chilli powder and serve immediately. *Serves 4*
Note: Many people think that a curry has to be swimming with sauce. This is not so, as many Indians have a taste for dishes free of excessive juice. However, it must be remembered that lack of liquid tends to concentrate the spices, therefore be very careful when altering the liquid quantity in recipes.

Prawn Curry with Coconut

Jhinga ka Pathia

75 g (3 oz) ghee
1 large onion, peeled and thinly sliced
2 cloves garlic, peeled and thinly sliced
7.5 cm (3 inch) piece fresh root ginger, peeled and thinly sliced
5 cm (2 inch) cinnamon stick
1 bay leaf
2 teaspoons chilli powder
2 teaspoons garam masala
1 teaspoon fenugreek seeds
1½ teaspoons salt
1 teaspoon freshly ground black pepper
225 g (8 oz) natural yogurt
175 g (6 oz) tomato purée
500 g (1 lb) peeled prawns
50 g (2 oz) desiccated coconut
chopped fresh coriander leaves (optional)

Melt the ghee in a large, heavy-based saucepan, add the onion, garlic and ginger and fry gently for 4 to 5 minutes until soft. Add the cinnamon and bay leaf, stir for 1 minute, then add the chilli powder, garam masala, fenugreek seeds, salt and black pepper. Stir well and fry for a further 2 minutes.

Stir in the yogurt and tomato purée. Increase the heat, add the prawns and any juices and stir to make a fairly thick sauce. (You may have to add a little water to prevent the mixture from becoming too dry.) Simmer for 2 minutes, then add the desiccated coconut and cook for a further 5 minutes, stirring carefully to ensure that the prawns do not break up. If wished, garnish with a sprinkling of chopped coriander leaves. *Serves 4 to 6*
Note: This dish comes from the south-west coast of India, where prawns are caught using an ingenious method involving the letting down of counterbalanced nets which trap fish and shellfish as they swim in and out with the tide. As the tide turns the nets are lifted out of the water to harvest the catch. In the West it is possible to pay quite considerable sums for large prawns, but there is little point in using them in this recipe as the result is very much the same with the smaller prawns.

Baked Fish

Tali Muchli

1 kg (2–2¼ lb) plaice or sole, cleaned but left whole
juice of 2 lemons

Coconut masala:
1 fresh coconut
5 fresh green chillies, cored and seeded
2 cloves garlic, peeled
2 tablespoons vegetable oil
2 tablespoons chopped fresh coriander leaves
1 tablespoon clear honey
2 teaspoons ground cumin
2 teaspoons ground fenugreek
1 teaspoon salt
1 teaspoon freshly ground black pepper

Wash the fish well under cold running water, then pat dry with paper towels. Place the fish on a plate, sprinkle over half of the lemon juice and set aside while making the coconut masala.

Make holes in the eyes of the coconut and drain out the liquid. Crack open the coconut and separate the meat from the shell. Place the meat in a blender or food processor and purée until smooth. Add the chillies, garlic and vegetable oil and purée again until evenly mixed, then add the remaining lemon juice, the chopped coriander, honey, cumin, fenugreek, salt and black pepper. Mix well to blend.

Spread this masala over the fish, turning it so that all sides are coated. Place the fish on a baking tray, cover with foil and bake in a preheated moderately hot oven (190°C/375°F, Gas Mark 5) for 25 minutes or until cooked through. Remove the foil and transfer the fish to a warmed serving platter. Serve hot. *Serves 6*
Note: This dish is typical of southern India, where freshly caught fish are often coated with a fresh coconut masala. Traditionally, the cooking is done on an open beach fire, either directly on grey dying embers, or on a flat, heated stone, but a conventional oven gives equally good results.

Apart from plaice or sole, any other flat fish could be used, or steaks cut from a larger fish such as cod.

Prawn Curry with Coconut; Spinach with Prawns (page 24); Madras Dry Prawn Curry

Charcoal-grilled Fish

Tandoori Muchli

1–1.5 kg (2–3½ lb) halibut, cleaned and washed
juice of 1 lemon
2 teaspoons salt
1½ teaspoons freshly ground black pepper

Masala:
1 large onion, peeled
1 clove garlic, peeled
1 tablespoon chopped fresh coriander leaves
4 teaspoons natural yogurt
2 teaspoons garam masala
1 teaspoon chilli powder
1 teaspoon ground coriander
1 teaspoon ground cumin
1 teaspoon ground fenugreek

Select a baking dish which is large enough to take the whole fish, then line with a sheet of foil 2½ times the size of the fish itself. Make 4 or 5 deep cuts in both sides of the fish. Rub the lemon juice on the fish and sprinkle with the salt and pepper. Place the fish on the foil and set aside.

To make the masala, place the onion and garlic in a blender or food processor and chop finely. Place in a bowl with the chopped coriander leaves, yogurt, garam masala, chilli powder, coriander, cumin and fenugreek. Mix well, then smear over the fish and inside the cuts and the cavity. Draw up the sides of the foil to make a tent shape, fold over and seal. Leave to marinate in a cool place for at least 4 hours.

Bake the fish in a preheated moderate oven (160°C/325°F, Gas Mark 3) for 20 minutes. Carefully remove the fish from the foil, place on a wire mesh and finish cooking over a charcoal barbecue. Care is obviously needed at this stage; if the fish is already over-cooked, there is a risk that it will break up when it is transferred to the barbecue. If preferred, finish cooking on a wire rack by the oven method. *Serves 4*

Note: Traditionally, a freshly caught fish is rubbed with masala, wrapped in a banana leaf and cooked in the ashes of a fire. This process, that combines baking and steaming in the banana leaf, traps the juices given off by the fish. Using foil is equally successful.

Baked Spiced Fish

Masala Dum Machchi

300 ml (½ pint) natural yogurt
1 medium onion, peeled and chopped
1 clove garlic, peeled and chopped
1 tablespoon vinegar
1½ teaspoons ground cumin
pinch of chilli powder
1 kg (2 lb) fish, cleaned, or 750 g (1½ lb) fish fillets
juice of 1 lemon
1 teaspoon salt

To garnish:
1 lemon slice
fresh coriander leaves

Put the yogurt, onion, garlic, vinegar and spices in a blender or food processor and purée until smooth.

Score the fish and place in an ovenproof dish. Rub with the lemon juice and sprinkle with the salt. Pour over the yogurt marinade, cover and leave to marinate in the refrigerator overnight.

Cover the fish with foil and bake in a preheated moderate oven (180°C/350°F, Gas Mark 4) for 30 minutes. Transfer to a warmed serving platter. Garnish with the lemon slice and coriander leaves before serving. Serve hot. *Serves 4*

Note: Any variety of fish, either whole or fillets, can be used for this tandoori-style dish, although white fish – such as sole or haddock – is preferable. If oily fish is used, double the quantity of vinegar.

Curried Crab

Kaleacha Kari

1 fresh coconut
600 ml (1 pint) boiling water
75 g (3 oz) ghee
1 large onion, peeled and thinly sliced
4 cloves garlic, peeled and thinly sliced
7.5 cm (3 inch) piece fresh root ginger, peeled and thinly sliced
2 teaspoons fenugreek seeds
2 teaspoons black or white peppercorns
2 teaspoons chilli powder
2 teaspoons ground coriander
1 teaspoon turmeric
1 teaspoon salt
500 g (1 lb) natural yogurt
300 ml (½ pint) milk
500 g (1 lb) frozen crab meat, defrosted
2 tablespoons chopped fresh coriander leaves, to garnish

Make holes in the eyes of the coconut, then drain out the liquid and reserve. Crack open the coconut and separate the meat from the shell. Thinly slice one-quarter of the coconut meat and set aside. Put the remaining three-quarters of the coconut meat in a blender or food processor and chop very finely.

Transfer the chopped or grated coconut to a bowl, pour over the boiling water, stir for 5 minutes, then strain through a sieve lined with a double thickness of muslin held over a bowl. Gather up the muslin and squeeze out as much of the coconut milk as possible. Discard the coconut from inside the cloth. Stir the reserved liquid from the coconut into the coconut milk and set the bowl aside.

Melt the ghee in a large, heavy-based saucepan, add the onion, garlic and ginger and fry gently for 4 to 5 minutes until soft. Add the fenugreek seeds, peppercorns, chilli powder, coriander, turmeric and salt. Stir well and fry for 2 to 3 minutes, then add the coconut milk. Put the yogurt and fresh milk in a bowl and stir together until evenly mixed. Stir slowly into the pan, bring to just below boiling point and then simmer for 5 to 6 minutes.

Add the crab meat and sliced coconut, folding the crab in gently so that the large pieces do not break up. Cook gently for a further 5 minutes, then turn into a warmed serving dish and sprinkle with the chopped fresh coriander leaves. Serve immediately. *Serves 6*

Barbecued King Prawns

Tandoori Jhinga

1 kg (2–2¼ lb) king prawns
juice of 2 lemons
1½ teaspoons salt
1½ teaspoons freshly ground black pepper
1 teaspoon aniseed

Marinade:
2 teaspoons coriander seeds
2 teaspoons fenugreek seeds
seeds of 20 cardamoms
1½ teaspoons black onion seeds (kalonji)
4 bay leaves
1 large onion, peeled and chopped
3 cloves garlic, peeled and chopped
7.5 cm (3 inch) piece fresh root ginger, peeled and chopped
350 g (12 oz) natural yogurt
1½ teaspoons turmeric
100 g (4 oz) ghee, melted
few drops of red food colouring

Wash the prawns and peel them, if wished. Alternatively, split the undersides with a sharp knife and slightly flatten them. Put the prawns in a bowl and sprinkle with the lemon juice, salt and pepper. Mix well, then set to one side.

To make the marinade, spread the coriander, fenugreek, cardamom and black onion seeds on a baking tray. Add the bay leaves and roast in a preheated moderately hot oven (200°C/400°F, Gas Mark 6) for 10 to 15 minutes. Cool, then grind with a mortar and pestle. Place the onion, garlic and ginger in a blender or food processor with the yogurt and turmeric and purée until smooth. Add the ground roasted spices and ghee and blend again for 30 seconds. Add the food colouring.

Pour the marinade over the prawns, then cover and marinate in the refrigerator for 3 to 4 hours if the prawns are peeled, otherwise overnight. Remove the prawns from the marinade, thread on to skewers and sprinkle over the aniseed. Barbecue gently for about 3 to 5 minutes or until cooked, turning frequently and brushing with the marinade. Serve hot. *Serves 4 to 6*

Steamed Mussels

Teesryo

1 kg (2–2¼ lb) mussels or clams
100 g (4 oz) ghee
1 large onion, peeled and finely chopped
2 cloves garlic, peeled and finely chopped
2 teaspoons desiccated coconut
2 teaspoons salt
1 teaspoon turmeric
1 teaspoon chilli powder
1 teaspoon freshly ground black pepper
150 ml (¼ pint) vinegar
500 g (1 lb) natural yogurt
2 teaspoons garam masala
juice of 2 lemons, to finish

Scrub the shellfish well under cold running water and remove the beards. Place in a large bowl, cover with fresh cold water and leave the mussels or clams to soak for 20 to 30 minutes.

Meanwhile, melt the ghee in a large, heavy-based saucepan, add the onion and garlic and fry gently for 4 to 5 minutes until soft. Add the desiccated coconut and salt and continue frying until the coconut begins to brown. Add the turmeric, chilli powder and pepper; stir well and fry for a further 1 minute.

Drain the shellfish and discard any that are open, or that do not close when tapped sharply on the shell. Add the vinegar to the pan with the shellfish, cover with a tight-fitting lid and increase the heat so that the mixture boils. Cook over high heat for about 5 minutes until the shells open, shaking the pan. Remove from the heat.

Remove the empty half shells from the shellfish and discard. Arrange the shellfish on the half shells in a warmed serving bowl, layering one on top of the other. Pour the cooking liquid from the pan into a blender or food processor. Add the yogurt and garam masala, blend for 1 minute, then return to the saucepan and bring to just below boiling point. Pour over the shellfish and sprinkle with the lemon juice. *Serves 6*

Note: Traditionally, this dish is made with clams, but the recipe works equally well with mussels.

Coconut Fudge (page 62); Rice Cooked with Chicken (page 36); Curried Crab; Egg and Coconut Curry (page 19); Steamed Mussels

Ạccompaniments

Accompaniments to Indian food include both bread and rice as well as various yogurt and lentil-based sauces. Some of the sauces can be extremely hot, while others are gentle and cooling.

In some parts of India bread is eaten at every meal. It can be deep-fried, like Puri and Paratha; baked on a hot plate or griddle, like the Chapatti; or baked in the oven, like Naan, the flat leavened bread.

Rice

Chawal

½ cup long-grain rice (Basmati or Patna)
1½ cups water
pinch of salt
pinch of saffron threads (optional)

Wash the rice well in at least 3 complete changes of cold water (it may need to be washed more if the water continues to be clouded by rice dust particles). Drain the rice, then pick over to remove any stones.

Place the rice in a large, heavy-based saucepan and pour in the measured water, which should cover the rice well. Add the salt, bring to the boil and simmer, uncovered, until cooked. The secret of good rice cookery is not to simmer for a specified time, but to check the rice constantly during cooking by removing a few grains and biting them, and to stop the cooking process before it has gone too far. The rice is just right when there is just a hint of a hard centre to the rice grains. If you find that too much water has been absorbed before this point is reached, then add a little more, which should preferably be boiling, so as not to hold up the cooking. Drain the rice when cooked.

To colour and flavour rice: place a pinch of saffron threads in a large cup, pour on boiling water to cover and leave to infuse for 20 minutes. Strain the saffron-coloured water into the rice as it simmers. As saffron is expensive, an alternative and more economical way of colouring rice (and to a certain extent flavouring it) is to use turmeric (see note under Saffron Rice). Use ¼ teaspoon of turmeric for each ½ cup rice, adding it to the water during the cooking process. *Serves 1*

Saffron Rice

Kesari Chawal

175 g (6 oz) ghee
2 large onions, peeled and sliced
350 g (12 oz) Basmati or Patna rice
1 teaspoon cloves
4 cardamoms
1 teaspoon salt
1 teaspoon freshly ground black pepper
½ teaspoon saffron threads, soaked in 1 tablespoon boiling water for 30 minutes
750 ml (1¼ pints) boiling water
silver leaf (varak), to garnish (optional)

Melt the ghee in a large, heavy-based saucepan, add the onions and fry gently for 4 to 5 minutes until soft.

Wash the rice thoroughly, then drain. Add to the pan with the spices, salt and pepper, then fry for 3 minutes, stirring frequently.

Add the saffron with its liquid and stir well to mix. Add the water, bring to the boil, lower the heat and simmer for 15 to 20 minutes until cooked. Drain.

Transfer to a warmed serving dish and garnish with the silver leaf, if liked. Serve hot. *Serves 4*
Note: Saffron is the most delicate of condiments, unique if only for the fact that, although used in very small quantities, its power is unrivalled. Saffron threads come from the stamens of a type of crocus which grows on the temperate slopes of the Himalayan foothills. It is common throughout northern India, particularly in Nepal and Bhutan where it is used to colour the robes of Buddhist priests a deep yellow.

It takes 75,000 crocus blooms to make 500 g (1 lb)

saffron, but then this delicate spice can colour several thousand times its own weight. Today, synthetic food colouring or turmeric is often used in place of saffron, but there can never be any substitute for the flavour of the real spice.

Indian Salad

Salat

1 lettuce
1 teaspoon salt
1 teaspoon freshly ground black pepper
1 teaspoon chilli powder
4 tomatoes
½ cucumber
1 large onion, peeled
2 teaspoons coriander seeds
juice of 1 lemon
4 fresh green chillies (optional)
½ teaspoon paprika, to finish

Separate the lettuce leaves, then wash and pat dry with paper towels or a clean teatowel. Mix together the salt, pepper and chilli powder. Pile one lettuce leaf on top of another, sprinkling each one with a little of the spice mixture. When you have 5 or 6 leaves together, cut them crossways into 2.5 cm (1 inch) shreds.

Put the shredded spiced lettuce leaves in a large salad bowl. Chop the tomatoes and cucumber, add to the lettuce and toss gently to mix. Slice half of the onion into thin rings and coarsely chop the other half. Mix the chopped onion with the lettuce, tomatoes and cucumber.

Dry-fry the coriander seeds in a heavy-based frying pan, then crush coarsely in a mortar and pestle. Mix the crushed seeds into the mixed salad and sprinkle with the lemon juice.

Arrange the onion rings over the top of the salad. Top and tail the chillies (if using), core and remove the seeds then chop into 5 mm (¼ inch) pieces and sprinkle on top of the onions.

Chill the salad in the refrigerator and sprinkle with the paprika before serving. *Serves 8 to 10*
Note: Indian salads are invariably chopped and mixed with various spices, some of them quite hot. This recipe is not too hot, although it does call for the inclusion of chopped fresh green chillies. Their use is optional. Almost any combination of vegetables can be used in this salad. Try Chinese leaves instead of lettuce and celery in place of the cucumber.

Mint-flavoured Sauce (page 51); Saffron Rice; Yogurt with Cucumber (page 53)

Poppadoms; Fried Unleavened Bread; Lentil Sauce with Hot Topping (page 23);
Saffron Rice (page 48); Leavened Bread with Poppy Seeds

Poppadoms

500 g (1 lb) red lentils or lentil flour (urhad)
4½ teaspoons salt
1 tablespoon baking powder
250 ml (8 fl oz) tepid water
about 50 g (2 oz) ghee
2 teaspoons black peppercorns
vegetable oil for frying

If using lentils, grind them into a fine flour in a blender or food processor. Sift the lentil flour, salt and baking powder into a bowl and gradually add the tepid water to form a very firm dough.

Warm the ghee until melted. Knead the dough for at least 20 minutes, sprinkling it with enough melted ghee to prevent it sticking to the bowl. Crush the peppercorns, sprinkle them over the dough, then knead them in until evenly distributed.

Break the dough into about 20 pieces the size of golf balls. Roll out each piece very thinly, until about 15 cm (6 inches) in diameter. Stack them on top of each other, separating each one with a sheet of greaseproof paper, then dry them out in a preheated moderate oven (180°C/350°F, Gas Mark 4) for about 2 to 2½ hours. Store in an airtight tin; they will keep for several weeks.

To cook the poppadoms: pour oil into a deep, heavy-based frying pan to a depth of 2.5 cm (1 inch). Heat the oil until very hot (a small piece of poppadom will immediately start to sizzle and float to the surface when dropped into the pan). Fry the poppadoms two at a time in the hot oil, rotating them for 5 to 10 seconds as they cook, using a combination of slotted spoon and fish slice. Turn them over and fry for a further 5 to 10 seconds. Lift them out of the frying pan, allowing excess oil to drain back, then stack them on end (as in a toast rack) in a warm place until well drained. Ideally, poppadoms should be served within 1 hour of frying, but they can be kept crisp, or be re-crisped, in a hot oven. *Makes about 20*

Note: Virtually all the Poppadoms that are eaten in the West are imported from India; this is because they are notoriously difficult to make, and imported ones are inexpensive to buy. However, if you do wish to have a go at making them yourself, the above recipe is quick and straightforward.

Mint-flavoured Sauce

Tandoori Chatni

225 g (8 oz) natural yogurt
2 tablespoons vinegar
2 teaspoons honey
juice of ½ lemon
½ teaspoon salt
½ teaspoon freshly ground black pepper
½ teaspoon chilli powder
green food colouring (optional)
1 tablespoon chopped fresh mint

Put the yogurt in a serving bowl. Heat the vinegar and honey in a small saucepan until the honey has melted. Leave to cool, then mix into the yogurt. Add the lemon juice, salt, pepper and chilli powder and stir well.

If liked, add food colouring to give the chatni a very pale green colour, then mix in the chopped mint. Cover the bowl and chill for 1 hour before serving. *Makes about 300 ml (½ pint)*

Note: 'Chatni' is the general name given to any sauce or pickle-like accompaniment. Chatnis can range from very hot and fiery concoctions such as chilli chatni, which is made entirely from green and red chillies, to rather milder chatnis made from sweetened aubergine or, as in this case, mint and yogurt.

This chatni is good with tandoori dishes, particularly the drier ones such as Minced Beef on Skewers/Seekh Kebab (page 30).

Fried Unleavened Bread

Paratha

500 g (1 lb) chapatti flour (ata) or wholemeal flour
1 teaspoon salt
600 ml (1 pint) water
225 g (8 oz) ghee

Sift the flour and salt into a bowl, gradually add the water and mix to a firm dough. Knead the dough for at least 10 minutes, until it glistens and does not stick to the bowl. Cover the bowl with a wet cloth and leave in a cool place for 4 hours.

Warm the ghee until melted. Divide the dough into 4 to 6 balls and roll each one out on a floured board to a circle about 5 mm (¼ inch) thick. With a pastry brush, generously brush some of the melted ghee over the surface of a circle of dough. Starting at one side, roll the dough up to form a sausage shape. Take one end of the sausage and wrap it round to form a spiral. Roll this spiral out to a circle 5 mm (¼ inch) thick. Brush with more melted ghee and repeat the process 4 times. Finally, roll out the dough until slightly less than 5 mm (¼ inch) thick. Repeat with the remaining dough to make 4 to 6 Parathas altogether. Melt the remaining ghee in a heavy-based frying pan until fairly hot. Fry the Parathas until golden brown and crisp on both sides, turning once. Drain and serve immediately. *Makes 4 to 6*

Note: Paratha is easy to make and requires no special skills – in fact it is very hard to get a Paratha wrong! Plain Parathas can be eaten as an accompaniment. To make them into a more filling meal, stuff the breads with a mixture of potatoes and peas or spinach and potatoes.

Leavened Bread with Poppy Seeds

Naan

500 g (1 lb) strong plain white flour
1 teaspoon baking powder
1 teaspoon salt
2 eggs, beaten
300 ml (½ pint) milk
1 tablespoon honey
50 g (2 oz) ghee
2 tablespoons poppy seeds

Sift the flour, baking powder and salt into a bowl. Add the eggs and mix well. Warm the milk and honey gently in a saucepan until the honey has melted, then add gradually to the flour and egg mixture to form a dough. Knead well for 5 to 10 minutes.

Warm the ghee until melted. Divide the dough into 6 equal pieces, brush one with a little of the ghee and knead again. Form into an oval shape, about 1 cm (½ inch) thick. Pick up some of the poppy seeds with moistened hands and press them into the dough. Repeat with the remaining pieces and melted ghee to make 6 Naan altogether.

Arrange the Naan on baking sheets and bake in a preheated hot oven (220°C/425°F, Gas Mark 7) for about 10 minutes, until the bread is puffed, golden and slightly scorched. Alternatively, cook under an extremely hot grill for 1½ minutes on each side. Serve hot, straight from the oven or grill. *Makes 6*

Note: Naan is traditionally cooked on the walls of a clay oven (*tandoor*). Rolled-out dough is slapped on the inside of the oven wall, near the top where it cooks very quickly in the fierce heat. Special irons are used: one has a flat end to scrape the Naan from the wall, the other a hook to remove it from the oven. Watching Naan cooked in this traditional way is fascinating, as the baker has to know exactly when it is the right moment to remove the Naan from the oven and how to hook it without it dropping into the hot coals.

51

Savoury Unleavened Bread; Spiced Dressing (with Prawns)

Spiced Dressing

Sambal

50 g (2 oz) ghee
1 large onion, peeled and chopped
2 cloves garlic, peeled and chopped
2 fresh green chillies, cored, seeded and chopped
1 teaspoon turmeric
½ teaspoon ground ginger
½ teaspoon ground cumin
½ teaspoon chilli powder

Melt the ghee in a heavy-based frying pan, add the onion and garlic and fry gently for 4 to 5 minutes until soft. Add the chillies and spices and fry for a further 3 minutes, stirring constantly. Use as required. *Serves 4*
Note: Sambal is a typical recipe from southern India, and is usually served as an accompaniment to a main dish. This recipe is for a basic Sambal, which can be used on its own or with other ingredients added to it — freshly shredded lettuce or cabbage, for example. If you add 2 tablespoons coconut milk or fresh milk, this will make a Sambal sauce which can be used to coat prawns. Aloo Sambal, another accompaniment, is made by adding diced cooked potatoes to the basic Sambal dressing.

Unleavened Bread

Chapatti

350 g (12 oz) chapatti flour (ata) or wholemeal flour
¾ teaspoon salt
about 300 ml (½ pint) water

Sift the flour and salt into a bowl, then gradually add the cold water and mix to a firm dough.

Turn the dough out on to a lightly floured surface and knead well until smooth and elastic. Break the dough into 8 to 10 pieces, then form each piece into a ball. Roll out each ball of dough to a thickness of 3 mm (⅛ inch).

Dust an ungreased, heavy-based frying pan or griddle (preferably cast iron) with a little chapatti or wholemeal flour. Place the pan over the heat until very hot, then add a chapatti and cook for 3 to 4 minutes until blisters appear on the surface. Turn the chapatti over and cook for a further 3 to 4 minutes.

Remove the chapatti from the pan with tongs, then place under a preheated hot grill for a few seconds until black blisters appear and the chapatti swells up. Wrap immediately in a warm teatowel (to keep in the moisture) and place in a basket while cooking the remaining chapattis. Serve warm. *Makes 8 to 10*
Note: Chapattis are the easiest of the Indian breads to make, and they are probably the ones with which most people are familiar. They are in fact flat unleavened pancakes made with a wholemeal flour called *ata*. This flour is available at Indian food shops, and is also sometimes called *chapatti* flour. If you are unable to find it, ordinary plain wholemeal flour can be used equally successfully.

If you follow the instructions in the recipe for wrapping the Chapattis in a teatowel after cooking, you can make them an hour or two in advance.

Curry Sauce

100 g (4 oz) ghee
1 large onion, peeled and sliced
2 cloves garlic, peeled and sliced
1 teaspoon ground coriander
1 teaspoon turmeric
1 teaspoon chilli powder
½ teaspoon salt
1 teaspoon freshly ground black pepper
300 ml (½ pint) water
1 teaspoon garam masala

Melt the ghee in a heavy-based saucepan, add the onion and garlic and fry gently for 4 to 5 minutes until soft but not brown. Stir in the coriander, turmeric, chilli, salt and pepper, blending well. Add the water and bring to the boil, lower the heat and simmer for 10 minutes, stirring frequently.

Add the garam masala and simmer for a further 5 minutes before serving. Use hot as required. *Makes about 450 ml (¾ pint)*

Yogurt with Cucumber or Tomato

Raeta

225 g (8 oz) natural yogurt
7.5 cm (3 inch) piece cucumber, or 2 medium tomatoes
pinch of salt
½ teaspoon freshly ground black pepper
pinch of chilli powder, to garnish

Put the yogurt in a serving bowl, thinning it down with a little milk, if necessary. Cut the cucumber lengthways into thin strips. (If using tomatoes, quarter them, then cut each quarter in half.) Mix the cucumber or tomatoes into the yogurt, sprinkling with the salt and black pepper. Cover and chill in the refrigerator for 1½ hours. Garnish with the chilli powder just before serving. *Makes about 300 ml (½ pint)*
Note: Raeta is one of the most important accompaniments to Indian food, as it counteracts any hotness. Although this recipe calls for either cucumber or tomato, try experimenting with cold cooked potato, cut into cubes, or finely chopped onion. Serve with Chick Pea Flour Fritters/Pakoras (page 14) made by frying the batter in small lumps.

It is important to make sure that the yogurt is thin; ideally the consistency should be similar to that of warm pouring custard.

Savoury Unleavened Bread

Namak Pare

50 g (2 oz) ghee
100 g (4 oz) strong plain flour
½ teaspoon salt
1 teaspoon lovage or caraway seeds
25 g (1 oz) natural yogurt
2 tablespoons water
vegetable oil for shallow-frying

Melt the ghee in a small saucepan until almost smoking. Sift the flour and salt into a bowl, then stir in the lovage or caraway seeds. Pour the hot ghee on to the flour mixture and mix well. Add the yogurt and cold water and mix to a moist dough.

Knead the dough in the bowl for 5 to 10 minutes, then set aside to rest for 20 minutes or so. Turn the dough on to a work surface and roll out to a square about 2 cm (¾ inch) thick. Cut into about 12 cubes.

Heat a little oil in a heavy-based frying pan, then shallow-fry the cubes in batches for about 3 minutes until golden brown. Drain on paper towels and leave to cool before serving. *Makes about 12*
Note: This is a simple recipe for a very tasty snack. Part of its attraction comes from the inclusion of lovage or caraway seeds. Savoury Unleavened Bread may be stored in an airtight container for up to 1 week.

53

Deep-fried Wholewheat Bread

Puri

175 g (6 oz) chapatti flour (ata)
½ teaspoon salt
150 ml (¼ pint) water
50 g (2 oz) ghee or butter, melted
vegetable oil for deep-frying

Sift the flour and salt into a bowl. Gradually add the water and mix to a firm dough. Add the ghee or butter and knead it in well. Cover and leave to rest for 30 minutes.

Divide the dough into 8 to 10 pieces, about 2.5 cm (1 inch) in diameter, then form into balls. Roll out on a lightly floured surface to rounds, just less than 3 mm (⅛ inch) thick.

Heat the oil in a large, heavy-based pan until moderately hot or until a Puri immediately starts to sizzle when placed in the oil and starts to float near to the surface. Deep-fry the Puris one at a time, for about 1½ minutes or until they puff up and float to the surface, spooning oil over them as they fry. Remove from the pan with a perforated spoon, drain on paper towels and keep hot in the oven while deep-frying the remaining Puris. Serve hot. *Makes 8 to 10*
Note: A traditional Indian breakfast will often include Puris; they are eaten simply – with plenty of chutney. Many people send to the bazaar for them, rather than cook them at home, as they are more easily prepared in bulk. As with all Indian breads, the secret is to serve them piping hot.

Rice with Stock and Spices

Pilao

750 g (1½ lb) Basmati or Patna rice
100 g (4 oz) ghee
2 large onions, peeled and thinly sliced
4 cloves garlic, peeled and thinly sliced
2 × 7.5 cm (3 inch) pieces fresh root ginger
15 cloves
15 cardamoms
2 × 5 cm (2 inch) cinnamon sticks
2 teaspoons turmeric
2 teaspoons black peppercorns
2 teaspoons garam masala
1 teaspoon salt
1.2 litres (2 pints) hot chicken stock
100 g (4 oz) sultanas
50 g (2 oz) slivered blanched almonds

Wash the rice well, drain, then pick it over to remove any stones or other 'undesirable' objects.

Melt the ghee in a large, heavy-based saucepan, add the onions and garlic and fry gently for 4 to 5 minutes until soft. Peel the ginger and cut it into strips about 5 mm (¼ inch) wide and 5 cm (2 inches) long. Add to the pan and fry for a further 2 minutes. Add the cloves, cardamoms and cinnamon sticks, stir well to mix and fry for a further 1 minute. Add the turmeric, peppercorns, garam masala and salt and fry for a further 2 minutes, stirring constantly.

Add the rice and stir well to ensure it is coated with the spice mixture. Pour in the hot stock and bring to the boil. Boil gently, uncovered, until the rice is just hard in the centre, stirring from time to time to ensure that it does not stick to the bottom of the pan. If necessary, add a little more hot stock or water.

When the rice is ready, pour it into a large sieve and allow any liquid to drain away. Transfer the rice to a large oval platter and sprinkle over the sultanas and almonds. Serve immediately, or keep hot in a moderate oven (180°C/350°F, Gas Mark 4) until ready to serve. *Serves 6 to 8*
Note: For many people, rice is a very difficult dish to get right. The method of cooking rice on page 48 should cause few problems, and the recipe given here is safe for beginners and newcomers to rice cooking, as the addition of ghee tends to prevent the grains of rice sticking together.

If wished, garnish with slices of tomato and hard-boiled egg just before serving.

Fried Chick Pea Flour Bread

Besani Roti

225 g (8 oz) chick pea flour (besan)
1 teaspoon salt
200 ml (⅓ pint) water
100 g (4 oz) ghee
175 g (6 oz) butter, melted

Sift the flour into a bowl, rubbing the lumps through the sieve with the back of a spoon. Stir in the salt. Gradually add the water and mix to a firm dough, then knead in the ghee and work until smooth.

Divide the dough into 4 to 6 pieces, each about 7.5 cm (3 inches) in diameter, then form into balls. Roll out on a lightly floured surface to a 5 mm (¼ inch) thickness.

Spread a little of the melted butter over the bottom of a heavy-based frying pan, then cook the Rotis one at a time, over a low heat, for about 3 minutes on each side. Transfer to an ovenproof plate and keep warm in the oven while cooking the remainder. Serve hot, brushed with the remaining melted butter. *Makes 4 to 6*
Note: This is a kind of fried bread which has an irresistible taste. *Besan* is a flour made from chick peas and its properties are therefore somewhat different from ordinary wheat flour. It is more aromatic and less starchy. It is also quite difficult to knead into a smooth dough, but this is essential for a good result.

Deep-fried Wholewheat Bread; Fried Chick Pea Flour Bread; Fried Unleavened Bread (page 51)

55

Chick Pea Flour Bread with Spinach

Saag Roti

500 g (1 lb) chick pea flour (besan)
2 teaspoons freshly ground black pepper
1½ teaspoons salt
4 tablespoons chopped fresh coriander leaves
300 ml (½ pint) milk
4 fresh green chillies, cored, seeded and cut into
5 mm (¼ inch) pieces
2 teaspoons caraway seeds
12 fresh young spinach leaves, hard central
stems removed
50 g (2 oz) ghee
melted butter, to serve

Sift the chick pea flour into a bowl together with the black pepper and salt. (The flour tends to form quite hard lumps; these need to be pressed through the sieve with the back of a spoon.) Mix in the chopped coriander. Gradually add the milk, mixing well to make a firm dough. Knead for at least 10 minutes, then leave the dough to rest in a cool place for 4 hours.

Knead the dough once again, sprinkling in the chillies and caraway seeds. Form the dough into 6 balls then roll each ball into a circle about 1 cm (½ inch) thick. Take 2 spinach leaves and lay them on top of 1 circle of dough. Fold the dough in half, form into a ball and roll out again into a circle about 1 cm (½ inch) thick. Repeat this process with the remaining spinach leaves and circles of dough.

Melt the ghee in a deep, heavy-based frying pan and shallow-fry the bread until brown on each side. Cut each circle of bread into wedges and serve piping hot, covered with melted butter. *Makes 6*
Note: The nearest Western equivalent to this particular snack would be a slice of pizza. This Eastern recipe is every bit as tasty.

Ḍesserts & Ṣweets

Desserts and sweetmeats are very popular in India and are not restricted to traditional mealtimes. Many sweets can be served at any time of the day but are particularly welcome with afternoon tea. Apart from the various flour-based confections, which are similar to some Western cakes, Indian cooks have perfected many exotic recipes which make use of concentrated milk or *khoa*. The procedure for making *khoa* is very laborious and today full-fat milk powder is used instead. The flavour of the finished sweet is just as good.

56

Sweet Rice

Kesar Pilau

500 g (1 lb) Basmati or Patna rice
350 g (12 oz) ghee
175 g (6 oz) sultanas
100 g (4 oz) shelled pistachio nuts
100 g (4 oz) blanched almonds
10 cloves
10 cardamoms
2.5 cm (1 inch) cinnamon stick
1 teaspoon ground allspice
1 teaspoon saffron threads, soaked in 1 tablespoon
boiling water for 30 minutes
900 ml (1½ pints) boiling water
100 g (4 oz) sugar
silver leaf (varak), to decorate

Wash the rice thoroughly, then put in a bowl and cover with cold water. Leave to soak for 2 hours.

Melt 100 g (4 oz) of the ghee in a large, heavy-based saucepan, add the sultanas and nuts and fry gently for 3 minutes. Remove from the pan with a perforated spoon and drain on paper towels. Set aside.

Melt the remaining ghee in the pan. Add the cloves, cardamoms, cinnamon and allspice and fry gently for 5 minutes, stirring frequently. Drain the rice, add to the spice mixture and mix well. Stir in the saffron with its liquid, then the boiling water.

Cover the pan and simmer for 20 to 25 minutes until the rice is tender and has absorbed the liquid. Drain off any excess liquid if necessary, then add the sugar and fried sultanas and nuts. Serve hot or cold, decorated with silver leaf. *Serves 4*
Note: This dish can be made richer by adding more fruit or nuts, or both. It is traditionally served on special feast days in India.

Creamed Rice Pudding

Kheer

600 ml (1 pint) milk
100 g (4 oz) sugar
50 g (2 oz) rice flour
2 teaspoons chopped pistachio nuts
2 teaspoons blanched slivered almonds
½ teaspoon rose water

Put the milk in a large, heavy-based saucepan and bring to the boil. Stir in the sugar, then sprinkle in the rice flour, stirring constantly. Add the nuts and cook until the mixture begins to thicken, stirring constantly.

Coconut Pudding; Creamed Rice Pudding; Sweet Rice

Remove the pan from the heat and stir in the rose water. Allow to cool. Serve cold. *Serves 4*

Note: At any Muslim festival — such as Id-Ul-Fitr — which is held to celebrate the end of a month of fasting — certain sweet dishes prevail. Muslims wear their best clothes and visit friends, where they will be invited to take tea and either of the traditional sweet dishes — Sewian or Kheer.

Kheer is based on rice flour, which is not always easily obtainable; it can however be made at home, by simply grinding rice in a coffee mill, blender, food processor or by using a mortar and pestle.

Coconut Pudding

Beveca

2 fresh coconuts
450 ml (¾ pint) boiling water
225 g (8 oz) caster sugar
175 g (6 oz) rice flour
2 eggs, beaten
50 g (2 oz) slivered almonds

Make holes in the eyes of the coconuts, then drain out the liquid and reserve. Crack open the coconuts and separate the meat from the shells. Grate the meat into a bowl, then pour on the boiling water. Leave to stand for 15 minutes, then strain the liquor through a sieve lined with a double thickness of muslin held over a bowl. Gather up the muslin and squeeze out as much of the coconut milk as possible. Discard the coconut from inside the cloth. Mix the strained coconut milk with the liquid extracted from the whole coconuts, then beat in all the remaining ingredients.

Put the mixture in a large, heavy-based saucepan and bring to the boil. Lower the heat and simmer until the mixture thickens, stirring constantly. Pour into a greased 20 cm (8 inch) round baking tin and bake in a preheated moderate oven (180°C/350°F, Gas Mark 4) for about 30 minutes until the top is browned. Serve hot. *Serves 4*

Indian Ice Cream with Pistachios

Pista Kulfi

300 ml (½ pint) double cream
300 ml (½ pint) milk
1 × 400 g (14 oz) can condensed milk
1 tablespoon clear honey
2 tablespoons chopped pistachios
2 teaspoons rose water
green food colouring (optional)

Heat the cream, milk, condensed milk and honey together in a heavy-based saucepan. Bring gently to the boil, stirring constantly, then simmer for 45 minutes over very low heat.

Remove the pan from the heat and sprinkle in the pistachios and rose water, then add a little food colouring, if using. Allow the mixture to cool.

Pour the mixture into a shallow 900 ml (1½ pint) freezer container or 6 to 8 *kulfi* moulds and freeze for 3 to 4 hours.

Remove from the freezer and leave to stand at room temperature for 20 to 30 minutes to soften. To serve, turn out of the *kulfi* moulds or cut into squares. *Serves 6 to 8*
Note: This is a very rich ice cream. Traditionally Kulfi is served from conical moulds.

Cream Cheese in Sweet Cream Sauce

Ras-O-Malai

Ras:
1.2 litres (2 pints) full-cream milk
juice of 2 lemons
100 g (4 oz) semolina
1 tablespoon chopped blanched almonds
1 tablespoon honey

Syrup:
1 litre (1¾ pints) water
6 cardamoms
6 cloves
7.5 cm (3 inch) cinnamon stick
175 g (6 oz) clear honey

Malai:
150 ml (¼ pint) milk
300 ml (½ pint) double cream
1 teaspoon rose water
1 tablespoon chopped pistachios

To make the *ras*, heat the milk in a heavy-based saucepan, add the lemon juice and bring to the boil. (The milk will curdle.) Continue to boil for a further 5 to 10 minutes. Leave to cool, then drain off the whey, leaving the curds behind. Place the curds in a double thickness of muslin, tie up and place in a sieve. Top with a weight to help remove the moisture. Leave overnight.

The next day, mix the resulting cheese (*panir*) with the semolina to form a dough, then break into 12 to 16 pieces the size of golf balls. Roll to a smooth ball shape, make a small indentation in the top of each ball and add a pinch of chopped almonds and a little honey. Re-form the balls, ensuring that the mixture is sealed inside. Set aside in a cool place.

To make the syrup, bring the water to the boil in a heavy-based saucepan together with the cardamoms, cloves and cinnamon stick. Lower the heat, add the honey and stir until melted. Increase the heat and boil rapidly, without stirring, until reduced to a syrup, three-quarters of the original volume. Gently add the cream cheese balls to the syrup and poach lightly for 1 hour 20 minutes. Remove the balls carefully with a perforated spoon, leave to cool, then chill in the refrigerator for about 2 hours.

To make the *malai*, boil the milk in a heavy-based saucepan until reduced to two-thirds of its original volume. Leave to cool, then stir in the double cream and sprinkle in the rose water and pistachios. Leave to cool, then chill in the refrigerator before pouring over the cream cheese balls. Allow to soak for several hours before serving. *Serves 6 to 8*
Note: This is one of the most delicious of all the Indian puddings. It is rich beyond belief.

Fried Bread in Saffron and Pistachio Sauce

Shahi Tukra

1 small loaf white bread, crusts removed
vegetable oil for deep-frying
1 teaspoon saffron threads
600 ml (1 pint) milk, warmed
225 g (8 oz) clear honey
50 g (2 oz) shelled pistachios, coarsely chopped
25 g (1 oz) blanched almonds, chopped
300 ml (½ pint) single cream
5–6 drops rose water

Cut the bread into 2.5 cm (1 inch) thick slices, then cut each slice lengthways. Heat the oil in a deep-fat fryer until hot and deep-fry the bread until golden, about 2 minutes. Drain and keep hot.

Put the saffron in a cup and cover with some of the milk. Add the honey to the remaining milk and heat until melted, then add the nuts. Strain in the saffron-coloured milk, stir well and remove from the heat. Cool slightly.

Stir in the cream and rose water. Put the bread in a serving bowl, pour over the sauce and chill in the refrigerator for at least 1 hour before serving. *Serves 6*
Note: This is very much a king of Mogul recipes. Although rich, it is refreshing to eat at the end of a large feast, when served chilled.

Cream Cheese in Sweet Cream Sauce; Indian Ice Cream with Pistachios;
Deep-fried Milk Pastry in Thick Syrup

Deep-fried Milk Pastry in Thick Syrup

Gulab Jamun

1 litre (1¾ pints) milk
juice of 2 lemons
100 g (4 oz) semolina
vegetable oil for deep-frying

Syrup:
300 ml (½ pint) water
5 cardamoms
5 cloves
225 g (8 oz) sugar
2 teaspoons rose water

Heat the milk in a large, heavy-based saucepan, add the lemon juice and bring to the boil. (The milk will curdle.) Continue to boil for a further 5 to 10 minutes. Leave to cool, then drain off the whey, leaving the curds behind. Place the curds in a double thickness of muslin, tie up and place in a sieve. Top with a weight to help remove the moisture. Leave overnight.

The next day, mix the resulting cheese (*panir*) with the semolina to form a dough, then break into about 15 pieces the size of unshelled hazelnuts. Form into smooth balls. Heat the oil in a deep-fat fryer until a ball of dough immediately starts to sizzle and float to the surface when dropped into the pan. Deep-fry the balls, in batches, until golden brown, then remove with a perforated spoon and drain on paper towels. Keep warm in a low oven.

To make the syrup, bring the water to the boil in a heavy-based saucepan together with the cardamoms and cloves. Lower the heat, add the sugar and stir until dissolved. Increase the heat and boil rapidly, without stirring, until the syrup starts to thicken. Allow to cool slightly, then sprinkle in the rose water. Put the pastry balls in a serving bowl and pour over the syrup. Serve warm. *Serves 4 to 6*

Note: These are very sticky, but flavoursome, Indian sweetmeats. Gulab Jamun should be eaten fresh to be enjoyed at their best, although they will keep in their syrup for several days if chilled in the refrigerator.

Mango Ice Cream

Am ka Kulfi

400 g (14 oz) canned mango pulp
3 tablespoons clear honey
600 ml (1 pint) double cream
50 g (2 oz) ground almonds
4 egg whites

Warm the mango pulp in a saucepan and stir in the honey until melted. Remove from the heat and stir in the cream and almonds until evenly mixed. Leave the mixture to become cool.

Pour the mixture into a freezer container and place in the freezer. Freeze for about 4 hours, or until the mixture is just beginning to freeze around the edges and become slushy. Remove the container from the freezer and turn the ice cream into a bowl. Break up with a fork.

Whisk the egg whites until stiff, then fold into the half-frozen mixture. Return to the freezer container and freeze again for a further 4 hours, or until solid. Remove from the freezer at least 20 minutes before serving to soften slightly. Serve sliced or scooped into chilled glasses. *Serves 8*
Note: This is a very rich, but refreshing, dish which combines the aromatic flavour of mangoes with the richness of cream. In India, a rather poor-quality cream known as *malai* would be used, but fortunately in the West the cream is better quality and therefore makes Kulfi even richer. This recipe can be made using fresh mangoes, but it is easier to use canned mango pulp, and there is no noticeable difference in the flavour of the ice cream. If canned pulp is not available, use canned mango slices and liquidize them in a blender or food processor. Because of the richness of Kulfi, rather smaller portions than normal are served.

Spiced Fruit Salad

Chaat

2 oranges
2 pears
1 eating apple
2 guavas
2 bananas
juice of 1 lemon
1 teaspoon ground ginger
1 teaspoon garam masala
½ teaspoon freshly ground black pepper
salt

Peel the oranges and divide into segments, removing all pith and pips. Peel, quarter and core the pears and apple, then cut into thick slices. Peel the guavas and cut into chunky slices, including the seeds. Peel the bananas and slice thinly.

Put the fruit in a serving bowl and sprinkle over the lemon juice. Mix together the spices and salt, then sprinkle over the fruit. Fold very gently until each piece of fruit is coated in the lemon and spice mixture, then cover the bowl tightly with cling film. Chill in the refrigerator for about 2 hours before serving. *Serves 4*
Note: Chaat is often served as an appetizer in India, or even as a cooling accompaniment to a hot main-course curry, but here it makes the most refreshing dessert.

In central and northern India it is a common sight to see stalls by the roadside selling Chaat and tea – an enjoyable combination which quenches the thirst and refreshes the body. All kinds of different fruits are used; the recipe above includes those that are readily available in the West, but you can vary the combination according to individual taste and what is in season.

Sweet Indian Pastries with Potato Filling

Meeta Samosa

225 g (8 oz) plain flour
pinch of salt
50 g (2 oz) ghee
warm water

Filling:
500 g (1 lb) potatoes, scrubbed
1 tablespoon chopped blanched almonds
seeds of 20 cardamoms
2 tablespoons clear honey
2 teaspoons sultanas
1 tablespoon chopped pistachios
vegetable oil for deep-frying

Sift the flour and salt into a bowl. Rub in the ghee, then add a little warm water to make a very firm dough. Roll into a large ball and set aside.

To make the filling, cook the potatoes in boiling water until just soft, about 20 minutes. It is important not to overcook the potatoes at this stage. Remove the skins from the potatoes, cut the flesh into 1 cm (½ inch) cubes and place in a bowl. Add the almonds and mix together.

Pound the cardamom seeds with a mortar and pestle. Warm the honey in a small saucepan so that it becomes very runny, sprinkle in the ground cardamom, then pour over the potato and almond mixture. Finally, sprinkle over the sultanas and pistachios.

To make the pastries, break the dough into 8 to 10 pieces the size of walnuts. Form into smooth balls. Roll out each ball on a floured surface to a very thin circle, about 1 mm (1/16 inch) thick. Place the circles of dough one on top of the other, with a light dusting of flour between each one. With a sharp knife, cut into 16 to 20 semicircles.

Place 2 teaspoons of filling on to one side of each semicircle, then fold the dough in a cone shape. Seal all the edges by moistening the dough with water. Heat the oil in a deep-fat fryer until hot, then deep-fry the Samosas, in batches, until they are crisp and light brown on all sides. Remove from the oil with a perforated spoon and drain on paper towels. Serve hot or cold. *Makes 16 to 20*

Note: Samosas are generally filled with a delicious savoury mixture, but this is a sweet version. In India, sweet Samosas are a classic teatime snack.

Vermicelli Pudding

Khir Sewian

100 g (4 oz) ghee
100 g (4 oz) vermicelli
750 ml (1¼ pints) milk
15 cardamoms
225 g (8 oz) clear honey
100 g (4 oz) sultanas

Melt the ghee in a large, heavy-based saucepan and add the vermicelli, breaking it into 10 cm (4 inch) pieces. Fry gently for 5 to 6 minutes, then pour on the milk and bring to the boil. Remove the seeds from the cardamoms, crush them in a mortar and pestle, then sprinkle into the pan. Add the honey, spoon by spoon, stirring well until melted. Cook for a further 10 to 15 minutes, then stir in the sultanas. Serve hot or chilled. *Serves 6*

Note: When Muslims visit each other, as is the tradition on Id-Ul-Fitr, they are always asked to partake of some food. Invariably, a large bowl of Khir Sewian is prepared, which is dipped into throughout the day as visitors come and go. It is not required for a guest to eat a great deal at one sitting; a small saucerful of Khir Sewian taken with a cup of tea is enough to show due respect for the hospitality.

Spiced Fruit Salad; Sweet Indian Pastries with Potato Filling

Honey Squares

Shehed Tukra

225 g (8 oz) self-raising flour
50 g (2 oz) ghee or butter
½ teaspoon grated nutmeg
pinch of ground cinnamon
150 ml (¼ pint) milk
vegetable oil for deep-frying
4 tablespoons clear honey
5 cm (2 inch) cinnamon stick
4 cloves
seeds of 4 cardamoms

Sift the flour into a bowl. Heat the ghee or butter gently in a saucepan and stir in the nutmeg and cinnamon. Add to the flour with the milk and mix to a firm dough with your fingers. Knead for at least 5 minutes.

Roll the dough to a thickness of 5 mm to 1 cm (¼ to ½ inch). Cut into 2.5 cm (1 inch) squares. Heat enough oil in a deep, heavy-based frying pan to cover the squares of dough. Add the squares and deep-fry until they are golden brown.

Meanwhile, put the honey in a clean saucepan with the cinnamon stick, cloves and cardamom seeds. Heat gently until the honey has taken the flavour of the spices, about 3 to 5 minutes.

Remove the cooked squares from the oil with a perforated spoon and drain quickly on paper towels. Arrange in a serving dish and strain over the honey syrup, discarding the whole spices. Leave to cool before serving. *Serves 6 to 8*
Note: These sweet honey squares are usually served as a snack in India, but they also make a good dessert for a special occasion. Like most pastries they are best eaten fresh, but will keep chilled in the refrigerator for up to 1 week.

Fudge

Barfi

350 g (12 oz) thick honey
150 ml (¼ pint) water
10 cloves
7.5 cm (3 inch) cinnamon stick
seeds of 20 cardamoms
175 g (6 oz) full-fat milk powder or baby milk formula
1 tablespoon chopped pistachios

Heat the honey gently in a large, heavy-based saucepan with the water until melted. Bring to the boil and add the cloves and cinnamon stick. Boil for 10 to 15 minutes, without stirring, to make a very thick syrup. If the syrup is not thick enough, boil it for a little longer. While the syrup is thickening, pound the cardamom seeds with a mortar and pestle, then transfer to a bowl, add the milk powder and stir well to mix.

Remove the syrup from the heat and sprinkle in the milk powder and cardamom seed mixture, stirring well to make a thick paste. Spread the mixture evenly in an ungreased fudge tin, about 20 cm (8 inches) square and 4 cm (1½ inches) deep.

Sprinkle the chopped pistachios over the top of the mixture and press them in lightly with the palm of your hand. With a sharp knife, make cuts in the mixture. Traditionally, a diamond shape is used, but the Barfi can be cut into any shape. Leave in a cool place until solidified, then remove from the tin before serving. *Makes about 750 g (1½ lb)*
Note: There are many different types of Indian sweets – all very rich and consisting mostly of sugar, milk and flavourings such as nuts, fruit and spices. Barfi is the general name given to a whole range of fudge-like sweetmeats.

The traditional method of making Barfi was so time-consuming, involving hours spent boiling down litres of milk, that Barfi was seldom prepared at home, but usually bought from professional confectioners. Resourceful Indian cooks have learnt how to make use of milk powder, and this has greatly simplified the making of Barfi.

Coconut Fudge

Narial ka Halwa

600 ml (1 pint) milk
100 g (4 oz) full-fat milk powder or baby milk formula
75 g (3 oz) desiccated coconut
½ teaspoon ground mace
2 tablespoons clear honey
50 g (2 oz) shelled almonds

Heat the milk in a non-stick saucepan until slightly warmer than tepid. Put the milk powder in a bowl and stir in enough of the warmed milk to make a smooth, thick paste.

Add the desiccated coconut to the milk remaining in the saucepan and bring to the boil. Continue to boil until most of the liquid has evaporated and the mixture is virtually dry.

Sprinkle in the ground mace and stir in the honey, then add the milk powder paste and stir well to mix. Continue to evaporate any remaining liquid until the mixture is very stiff.

Spread the mixture in a greased fudge tin, about 20 cm (8 inches) square and 2.5 cm (1 inch) deep. Leave to cool, then cut into the traditional diamond-shaped pattern with a sharp knife and decorate each piece with an almond. Remove from the tin before serving. *Serves 6 to 8*
Note: Most people in the West are familiar with coconut as the basis of a number of sweet confections, although many Indian recipes for Halwa are based on semolina – and there is even a version which uses grated carrots. This recipe makes a particularly rich sweetmeat; it will keep for several weeks if stored in an airtight container.

Carrot Pudding; Spiced Semolina Dessert

Spiced Semolina Dessert

Halwa

225 g (8 oz) semolina
4 tablespoons desiccated coconut
500 g (1 lb) sugar
1 tablespoon poppy seeds
seeds of 6 cardamoms
600 ml (1 pint) water
100 g (4 oz) ghee, melted

Put the semolina in a large, heavy-based saucepan with the coconut, sugar, poppy and cardamom seeds. Mix well then stir in the water. Bring to the boil, stirring constantly, then lower the heat and simmer for at least 1 hour until every ingredient is soft, stirring frequently. Gradually add the ghee and mix well to incorporate.

Transfer the mixture to a shallow tray and spread evenly. Leave to cool, then cut into triangles or diamond shapes. Store in an airtight container in a cool place. *Serves 4*

Note: There are as many Halwas in India as there are cities, and each centre of population guards the reputation of its sweetmeat.

Often Halwa is used as a kind of culinary envoy — being sent all over the world. It is well worth making at home, although it is said the art of the *halwai* (halwa-maker) is inherited and cannot be learnt!

Carrot Pudding

Gajjar Kheer

500 g (1 lb) carrots, peeled and grated
225 g (8 oz) sugar
1.5 litres (2½ pints) milk
6 cardamoms
1 tablespoon sultanas
1 tablespoon slivered almonds

Put the carrots in a bowl and sprinkle with the sugar. Set to one side.

Put the milk in a large, heavy-based saucepan with the cardamoms. Bring to the boil and boil steadily for 45 minutes or until the milk is reduced in quantity by half. Add the carrot and sugar mixture and simmer until the mixture thickens.

Remove the pan from the heat, leave to cool slightly, then stir in the sultanas and almonds. Serve hot or cold. *Serves 4*

Note: Carrots are not the usual kind of ingredient for a sweet pudding, but in this dish they are used with great effect. It is very rich and sweet, and few people will have room for a second helping!

Index